Bud

will

enjoy. Love,

Darlene and
John

Christmas,
2012

Dennis
Darres -

NATIVE AMERICAN TRAIL MARKER TREES
MARKING PATHS THROUGH THE WILDERNESS

DENNIS DOWNES

with Neal Samors
Foreword by Janet Davies

CHICAGO'S BOOKS PRESS

Native American Trail Marker Trees:
Marking Paths Through the Wilderness

Copyright ©2011 by Dennis Downes.

Published in the United States of America in 2011 by
Chicago's Books Press, an imprint of Chicago's Neighborhoods, Inc.

First Edition

Edited by Dennis Downes, Neal Samors and Elizabeth Anne Fox
Produced by Dennis Downes, Neal Samors and Elizabeth Anne Fox
Designed by Sam Silvio, Silvio Design, Inc.
Printed in Canada by Friesens Corporation

ISBN 13:9780979789281

Front Cover
Sculpture of 16 foot Trail Marker Tree in front of
Lake County Discovery Museum, Wauconda, Illinois.
Sculpture by author Dennis Downes.

Back Cover
Bronze plaque acknowledging an historic Indian Trail Marker
Tree on Canterbury Court in Wilmette, Illinois.

For more information on this book and the author's
artwork visit www.downesstudio.com or contact the author
at dennis@downesstudio.com.

This book is dedicated to my Mother, Mary Berriochoa Downes, who always encouraged me and believed in me and to my wife, Gail Spreen Downes, for all her help and understanding during the course of this project.

TABLE OF CONTENTS

ACKNOWLEDGEMENTS

A special thank you to some of the many who helped
to make this project possible

Meredith Anderson, Amy Amdur, George and Peggy Anton, Chris and Tracey Ano, Kathy Hussey Arnston, Frank and Bonnie Atkinson, Jan and John Bachmeier, Wayne Beck, Wendy Belmont, Larry Black, Amy Blue, John and Peggy Benandi, Lori and Ben Berriochoa, Luis Berriochoa, Mary Busch, Brian and Nadean Buchholz, Brenda Bogen, Donna and Don Brown, The Bies Family, Bob Bensmen, Albert and Martie Berriochoa, Debbie Berkowitz, Nancy Beattie, Mike and Teresa Baber, Blarney's Island, Eris Bonokoski, Art and Joyce Buehler, Jacky and Ward Budwig, Jim and Colette Broadway, Jeff and Terry Brizzorlaro, Barry Berish, Lee Block, Mike Berriochoa and Family, Wilma and Klaus Brauer, Patrick and Carmen Brauer, Darrell Baker, Gretchen and Brian Boyer, Loretta and Ralph Bunnell, Judith Baker, Ron Bernardi, Kole Berriochoa, Richard Bales, Mable Buckner and James Payton, Luke and Joanne Carlson, Ray and Suzanne Chrisler, Perry and Dale Crakes, Kevin and Darcy Creevy, Mike and Joan Collins, John and Ade Clark, Peggy and Sam Ciccarelli, Annie Cobb, Ted and Cindy Cartner, Linda Copell, Charlie and Ellie Clarke, Mary Cunningham and Wertz Family, Mike and Cheri Capello, Sue and Greg Cambell, Dean C. Dunn, Debbie at BP, Joe and Judy Dietz, Julie and Mike Dodds, Steve and Roseanne DeVitt, Dockers North, Rich and Dell Donahoe, Gary Donatelli and Family, Patrick and Kim Downes, Pat

and Meg Downes, Mike and Stephanie Downes, Harry and Vickie Downes, Jane and Donald Downes-Kirkpatrick, Mike and Velma Downes, Nancy, Kathy, Patty, Laura Downes and Families, Carol Davis, Carol DiLorenzo, Renee J. Drendel, Lou and Chris Downes, Dan and Breanna Downes, Maryann Downes, Heather Downes, John and Elizabeth Downes, Janet Davies, Reene and Richard Dankert, Patty Dodson, Sally and Larry Domont, Ray Ebner, Tom English and Family, John and Felicia Eberle, Paul Eubanks, Ken and Claudia Ferraro, Heidi and Joe Fornarotto, Gary and Cathy Frankowski, William Friese, Michael and Barbara Fulle, Bob and Lynette Foss, William Friese, Carol Ann Busche, Sue and Rich Gorley, Michael Gorman, Sue Graff, Marco Greco, Eddie G., Alex and Margaret Georgopulos, Nicholas and Stacey Geordan, Janet L. Gallimore, Trish and Dick Grey, Bill Gleespen, Lee Golub and Family, Bernie and Kelly Guntz, Michael Griem, Kevin Gibbons, John and Maureen Haling, Jack and Dawn Harry, Joan Hammel, Heydt Family, John and Laurin Heineman, Charles and Janice Herndon, Colleen and Mark Holohan, Holly Hoier, Judy Hughes, Scott Holmes, John Hykes, Jennifer Harris, Marsha Hestad, Leo and Kristin Hirsch, Rick and Janie Jerch, Dave Johnson, Jerry Johnson, The Lodge, George and Carolyn Joseph, Albert Joseph, Janelle Joseph, Gary and Cheri Jensen, Amy Jenkins, Ed and Mary,

Jim Jordan, Glenn Jones, Terry Kausch, Terry Hallett, Edith E. Hauff, Marlene Kebler, Janice and David Koza, Tom Kurowski, Deb Kozie, Kevin Kozie, Janice Kozie, Kathy LaBuda, Marty Karowsky, Don King, Mike and Kelly Kelly, Keith and Britney Kura, Rich and April King, Terrence R. Lyons, Helaine Lasky, Dave and Diane Lester, Helen and Arthur Landwehr, Patrick Leary, Jeannine and Jim Leffel, David and Heidi Lloyd, Michael and Kimberly Lynch, Gregory Mackey, Dolores Maldonado, Glenna Mangelsdret, Daniel Martin, Lynne Mace, Nanci and Mark Marshal, Robert P. McEvoy, The Meter Family, Howard and Pauline Morrison, Mark Mooradian, Clyde McFaul, Franklin McMahon and Family, Edward, Judy, and Mindy Michalak, Ann, Blackdog, Emily, and Charlie Miller, Mark Moose Mitchem, John and Linda Misek, Eric and Kathy Moberg, Stuart and Annette Munro, Matt Nagel, Janine and Richard Neff, Richard and Jody Neubiser, Pat Carroll and Gary Meyer, Linda Niecestro, Jim and Trisha Novac, Suzie and Jim Otterbeck, Bill, Linda, and Chuck Olson, Marty Olson, Jim O' Rourke, Barb and Pat Seng, John and Jill Payne, Scot and Lori Pepper, Bill Perdi, Betty Perik, Valerie Perron, Jim and Mary Pomerantz, Carole Pompa, Angelo Pope, Bill and Linda Appleton- Potter, Ann and Greg Prochnow, Betty Pauley, Linda Gartner Phillips, Captain's Quarters, Peter Quinn, Nancy and John Remington,

Dave and Laura Roberts, Glenn and Carolyn Roberts, Adam and Ellen Romeiser, Pam and Jon Rosen, Roy's Auto, Jennifer Richards, Frank Rumoro, Emma Russell, Gary and Julie Rusch, RIE, Kathy Robbinson, Jess Ray, The Sandbar Bar and Grille, Harry and Karly Spell, Katherine Hamilton-Smith, Bob and Connie Schneider, Don and Ken Schreiber, Keith and Pam Schultz, Cindy Schwab, Sue Schwabe, Jim and Barb Siano, Adrian and Nancy Smith, Robert Smith, Elroy Spreen, Lorna Spreen James Staib, Debbie Stannard, Art and Linda Staubitz, Joy and Judd Steinback, Mike and Cathy Steinback, Rick Steinback, Jeff and Patti Steinback, Louis Stauffer, Pat Strong, Adele and Bill Sturgis, Bob and Nina Swanson, Roger Shule, The Saffir Family, James Tichy, Ray and Tony Tonelli, Deidre Toner, Gail Trulson, Tim and Nora Tye, Tina and Taso, Tracy Patterson, Carol and Marty Tyskling, Pat Taylor, Helen Hornbeck Tanner, James Ulrich, Melodie Ustich, Patti Van Cleave, Kallen Vonrenken, Mark Vanden-Heuvel, Ainsley Wonderling, Howie W. Walz, Vince and Mary Waidzulis, Sprite Wacker, Webb's Marina, Bryan White, Kathy Weissmuller, Thomas and Vada Wheeler, Vincent White, Dennis and Lorise Weil, Lynn and Gary Wendt, Michael T. Wasielewski, Barney Wyckoff, Pam and Larry Zall, The Zenner Family, Steve Young, Steve and Holly Zeinfeld

FOREWORD

by Janet Davies

My sons and I call it the 'funky sittin' tree'. It's shaped like the pipe you would see under a sink.... a really big sink. The tree has a runny nose, literally. This sugar maple rests in quiet solitude on the back end of 19 acres my family owns in Michigan. Nearby are a small spring and a protected depression in the earth that we imagine to have once been a possible rest stop/camp ground along an ancient Native American 'roadway.' The Miami tribe reportedly once lived in the area. Located two miles from our property is US Highway 12, also known as part of the "The Old Sauk Trail," an ancient Indian route used for trade between Detroit and the Mississippi River. Currently, the Pokagon Band of the Potawatomi Nation continues a vital presence in this part of Michigan.

For the longest time, the tree was a marker for just us, a way of orienting ourselves in the woods when the summer foliage was dense. In winter, against the snow draped landscape, it was a touch of woodland art.

In fact, on a January weekend a few years back, our friend George Joseph was tramping with us through these woods when he stopped suddenly in front of this misshapen tree. Gazing in wonder, he proclaimed, "I think you have something quite old and historical right here. I know the guy who can tell you what this is!" Huh?

In less than a week, I met Dennis Downes and discovered why I had always felt a mystical sense of journey when I was near this tree... a deep spiritual connection to earth that is surprising for a woman with not a drop of Native American blood.

In my woods is a Potawatomi Trail Marker Tree.

Fighting against choking parasitic vines, bearing the scar of a lightning strike and housing a condo complex of various creatures, this soaring sentinel has been slumbering for nearly two centuries since its services were no longer needed. Our Trail Marker Tree did have to wake up and dodge chainsaws a few decades ago when a previous owner contracted a lumber company to clear cut much of the property. When you are an old bent gent and not offering up great board length, you get ignored. Whew!

I sometimes sit in front of it imagining a Native American family seeing my tree in the distance and knowing this is where they would stop. Our small spring would have given them water and they would rest protected in our camp site. When refreshed, perhaps their travel would take them to the big water of "Michi gami" less than a day's walk. For us, Lake Michigan is only a 20 minute car ride.

One and all who visit our Michigan land always are led in pilgrimage to the tree. Without fail, everyone has question. How was it made? (Read this book) In what direction is it pointing? (Slightly northwest) How old? (Possibly 200-250 years) To what was it pointing (Who knows? Lake Michigan? A Potawatomi village? Another rest area? A sacred spot?) Shouldn't you protect this tree? (We make sure it is kept private, Plus, I even bravely pull poison ivy from its bark) How long will it last? (Can't answer that)

The sad reality is these trail marker trees are rapidly disappearing. It's to be expected of a living thing, especially one ancient, neglected and under attack by man and nature. We are lucky there are still many standing and (fingers crossed) a number to still be discovered. It is Dennis Downes who is passionately working to document their history and give life to their story. Someone must tell it before the remaining Tree Trail Markers slowly give up their spirit and rejoin the earth.

INTRODUCTION

An Early Interest in the Subject

by Dennis Downes

I first became interested in the subject of the Trail Marker Trees as a young boy around the age of twelve. In the 50's when I was a child, I lived in an area between Wheeling and Northbrook in Illinois near the Des Plaines River, about seven miles west of Lake Michigan, with my older brothers Luis and Harold, younger brother Patrick, and younger sister Maryann. One day, I was walking near the lake when I saw a tree that I would soon learn was called a Trail Marker Tree. A man noticed that I was looking closely at the odd shaped tree and he took the time to explain that it wasn't just a deformity of the tree, but actually a Trail Marker Tree that had been shaped by the Native Americans. The man described what made Trail Marker Trees special and why they were important to the Indians. These trees had been used by American Indians throughout their history to mark trails. The man said that they could be found all over the United States and that this was just an example of one shaped here on the North Shore.

Dennis' grandmother, Celestina Berriochoa, and Uncle Al in the Bitterroot Mountains, Idaho.

Dennis' great grandfather, Ignacio Berriochoa, born 1864. One of the first Berriochoas to settle in Idaho.

Dennis and Linda Appleton Potter along the shores of the Salmon River near Sun Valley, Idaho. Dennis displayed part of his Trail Marker Tree exhibit and gave a private talk to Mr. and Mrs. Potter and a group of selected friends. Linda Appleton Potter is a member of the Board of the Sun Valley Center for the Arts and the Appleton Museum of Art Advisory Council. Photo taken by Gail Spreen.

Opposite
Dennis' grandfather, Adrian Berriochoa, born 1896, lived in Mountain Home, Idaho.

As I grew up, my playground was the local forest preserve and the Des Plaines River. Just by walking half a mile to the Des Plaines River, I could then walk through the forest along the river for miles in either direction. I soon learned that there was Indian lore to be learned and artifacts to be found all along the river and forest system.

Later, my heritage would play a large part in the way I viewed the Trail Marker Trees and Native American culture. Part of my early education was learning that my mother's people descended from the ancient Basque culture that originated in the Pyrenees Region of Europe. Most Americans do not know a great deal about the Basque culture; the Basque people were referred to as Europe's "First Family" by National Geographic. The Basques are also part of the very fabric of the Native American ancestry, according to the most recent concepts of the peopling of America.

My mother's family settled in Idaho over one hundred years ago. Although I grew up in the Chicago area, we visited my mother's people in the Rocky Mountain region on a regular basis. During these visits, I learned about the American Indians and began to appreciate the landscapes of the West; having an interest in the outdoors and Native Americans just seemed to come naturally. My mother, Mary Berriochoa, was raised in several small mountain towns throughout Idaho. Influenced by her surroundings growing up, she is truly a unique woman, her way of life stresses self-reliance, quick thinking, and a problem solving attitude.

During my childhood I was greatly influenced by many of my relatives. On my mother's side of the family, my uncle Luis Berriochoa, was an avid outdoorsman and competitive skier growing up in Idaho. As a young man he was honored by being accepted into the Army's 10th Mountain Division during World War II. He was also selected to become one of the ski instructors for the 10th Mountain Division. During the war he was wounded and received the Purple Heart and Bronze Star for his service. Upon his return from the war he continued to ski both recreationally and competitively; he often skied at Lookout Pass on the Montana-Idaho border. He later became Postmaster General in Mountain Home, Idaho. His father, my grandfather, Adrian Berriochoa owned and operated a night club in Mountain Home, Idaho, for over 40 years. It is still named after him to this day.

My mother's heritage can be traced back centuries in the Basque region of the Pyrenees. One of our ancestors was a Catholic missionary of the Dominican Order, who was martyred and later canonized. Saint Valentin Berrio-Ochoa was beheaded in Vietnam while serving as a missionary in the mid 1800's. He converted many Vietnamese to Catholicism. When he was beheaded, 116 other Vietnamese men went to their death with him; he is still honored there to this day. My Uncle Val, who died in the early sixties, was named after Saint Valentin. Val had a passion for aviation and soloed at the age of 16. By the age of 18, he had obtained his commercial and instructor ratings and prior to World War II was a flight instructor with the Civilian Pilot Training program. During the war he was a civilian flight instructor with the Army Air Corps, teaching advanced flying skills at bases in Texas and Missouri. His wife Elaine, who is now in her nineties, shared his passion for aviation, and in 1939, became the first woman in Idaho to earn a commercial rating. My mother's brother, Al, served in the Navy and is now a cross country truck driver, he is still driving today. Al and his wife currently reside in Alabama.

When we would visit my family in Idaho, it would usually take us at least four days to get there. The trip was truly an adventure because it would often include several flat tires, overheated radiators, and brake failures. The whole family packed into one car, never knowing where we would stay each night or who we would meet along the way. When we arrived in Idaho my uncles would take us target shooting in the mountains and hiking and fishing along the shores of the Snake River. It was always a thrill to see eagles, mountain lions, or bears. I still continue to visit Idaho on a regular basis to this day.

My paternal grandfather immigrated to this country by himself in the early 1900's from Ireland and settled in the Chicago area, first in the city and then on Cedar Island located on the Chain O'Lakes. My father's family had a passion for the outdoors; much of my time spent with them was spent outside. Many of my earliest memories are of fishing and boating on the Chain and the Fox River. As a boy, my father, Matt Downes, said I was always asking questions about everything, especially about the Native Americans and the history of our

A photo taken by Dennis of the
Coeur d'Alene River in Idaho.

"Downes' historically significant bronze sculpture of Saint Valentin Berrio-Ochoa was dedicated and installed into the Basque Museum and Cultural Center in Boise, leading to the Governor of the State of Idaho, C.L. "Butch" Otter, to officially proclaim July 29th, 2011 to be Saint Valentin Berrio-Ochoa Remembrance Day."

area. Some of the older residents who lived in the Chain O'Lakes region near my grandpa would tell me different stories about the area and about the trails they would take from Chicago that were old Indian routes to places such as Green Bay, Lake Geneva, and Galena.

My uncle John, who has since passed away at the age of 93, would always tell me about what he and the other relatives had done when they were younger. One family tradition was that when a boy became a teenager he would embark on an extended canoeing trip. My grandfather had three sons, Nicholas, John, and Matt, and he would allow them to chart out their canoe route in the Boundary Waters between the United States and Canada. They would plan a two-month trip along the Lake of the Woods and the Rainy River area.

Grandpa Downes would drive the boys towing his makeshift trailer with the canoes and gear to the beginning location of the trip. The boys were responsible for paying for their own canned goods and whatever little fishing gear they were going to bring. They were responsible for charting their course and making sure they had necessary first aid equipment. Grandpa had a copy of their map so he knew where the boys were going during the canoe trip.

Sixty days later, Grandpa would meet them at the prearranged destination with a change of clothes and a big meal from Grandma. Uncle John took this trip several times and told me that it actually helped him later to cope with the situations he faced during World War II; many of his early experiences

taught him self-reliance and perseverance. He received the Legion of Merit and five Bronze Stars for his service during the war as part of the 47th Armored Medical Battalion. Uncle John was a big influence in my life and I have great respect for him. Stories of trips and adventures like these between my Uncle Nick, Uncle John, and dad; whether by canoe, car, or motorcycle were what I listened to growing up.

On my father's side of the family; if a motor broke, they fixed it; if a boat had a hole in it they repaired it; if a seawall went down, they rebuilt it. Many of their efforts can still be seen on Cedar Island today. There was always a job to do and we, their children, were always their helpers. My father, Matt, was in the Air Corps during World War II; he never gave up on any project and always seemed to care about "the other guy."

When my father returned state side, he was stationed in Mountain Home, Idaho, where he met my mother. Once he was discharged and sent home to the Midwest, he would take motorcycle trips across the country to return to Idaho to see my mother, his drum majorette. The year he took his first motorcycle trip coincided with the first year that Sturgis Motorcycle Rally resumed after the war.

As a child, I first went to school in Northbrook at St. Norbert's Catholic Elementary School and then attended Glenbrook North High School. It was while I was in high school that I began to explore different forms of art. At Glenbrook, my main interests were art and sports, I was able to take many art courses. Guido Chigi, an oil painter

A photo of the bruneau dunes near Snake River Idaho, taken by Dennis. Dennis camped alone here for weeks.

Luis Berriochoa, Dennis' uncle, shown in 1942 as part of the 10th Mountain Division, the 85th Mountain Regiment. Camp Hale, Colorado.

Luis Berriochoa in Italy-1945– was wounded in northern Italy during battle.

Val Berriochoa, Dennis' Uncle, WWII Air Corps Flight Instructor.

Elaine McCalley Berriochoa, member of the Idaho Aviation Hall of Fame, Dennis' aunt and Val's wife. She was the first woman to receive a commercial pilot's license in Idaho.

and head of the art department at the high school, was my biggest artistic influence during this time. I am not sure Mr. Chigi knew what a significant influence he had on me. He was the one who suggested that I should paint what I believe in; he told me, "You won't be as popular early on, but, if you stick with it, you will be happier in the long run."

When I first developed an interest in the topic of Native Americans and their history, it was not limited to just my area. I also tried to study Indian tribes who had lived in the Western states near where my mother had grown up. When one of my aunts from Idaho visited us in Illinois, she took me to the Potawatomi Woods County Forest Preserve along the Des Plaines River and spent the day with me walking and talking. She told me, "Why don't you study this area first? It is rich in Indian lore and history. You can focus on your own area where you live first and then go from there." Taking my aunt's advice, that is exactly what I did and started to learn about the tribes in my area of the Great Lakes Region. I also began to develop an appreciation of artists like Remington, Russell, Catlin, and photographer Edward Curtis who brought to the forefront some of the symbolism of tribes that had been located in the West, Northwest, and Plaines areas.

After high school I attended Southern Illinois University, studying art, mainly painting. After leaving SIU, I moved 30 miles off of the Carbondale campus. The nearby Shawnee National Forest became my new classroom along

Dennis' aunt Adeline and uncle Albert on grandpa Adrian's horse in Shoshone Idaho.

Dennis, his brothers Luis and Harold, and mother Mary on their way to Idaho.

Dennis' uncle, John Downes with his friend Red Grange and wife Margaret (Muggs) at their home in Florida. Photo taken by Ruth Downes.

Capt. John Downes, active duty January 8th 1942– December 13th 1945.

This photo was taken during the installation ceremony of Dennis' 16' realistic Trail Marker Tree sculpture at the Lake County Discovery Museum in 2004. The Director of the Museum posed with Dennis and the many visitors and patrons around the sculpture.

with the Mississippi River, the Grand Tower, the Garden of the Gods, and the Big Muddy. Ironically, much later in life I would be revisiting these locations along the Mississippi River and searching for Trail Marker Trees as my study continued. In the early parts of my study of the Trail Marker Trees, very few people realized what I was trying to accomplish. Although some of my closest friends would join me to take canoe or hiking trips throughout the Midwest where the Trail Marker Trees were located, they often did not realize I was also searching for the trees.

While living in southern Illinois I learned, to some extent, what it is like to live with fewer amenities. We had to gather wood every day in the cold weather for the potbelly stove, some days we had running water and some days we did not. These experiences taught me to appreciate the simple things people take for granted. It is one thing to rough it for a weekend, but it is quite different to live like that every day.

After several years in the Carbondale area, I moved back to the northern Illinois area where I began living at The Grove, located on Milwaukee Avenue in Glenview, a place that today is a national landmark. The Grove was the original home of Dr. John Kennicott in the 1800's. In the early 1800s, Milwaukee Avenue was an Indian trail that later became a stage coach line. Later, I would learn there were many Trail Marker Trees located in and around The Grove. While I was living at The Grove, my interest in the outdoors, nature, and

the Native Americans was rekindled. The Grove was not a historic site at the time I was living there; at that time it was very run-down. It was later saved in the '70s, by a lobbying group known as the "Frog & Fern Ladies." They fought, and won, a skirmish to keep and preserve The Grove as the historical landmark it is today.

Unfortunately, in the early '70s not many people were aware of The Grove's historical significance. Since then, all that has changed due to the "Frog & Fern Ladies" and the Grove Heritage Association, director Steve Swanson, and his staff. Dr. John Kennicott was one of the first settlers in the Glenview area. His son, Robert, accomplished a great deal by the age of 30. Robert helped found the Chicago Academy of Sciences and contributed to the founding of the Historical Museum at Northwestern University. Later these two establishments would link directly into my Trail Marker Tree study. The Chicago Academy of Sciences had many members with interest in the Trail Marker Trees, including Charles Raddin and Jens Jensen. Frank Grover wrote one of the first papers on Trail Marker Trees in the Chicagoland area and referred to fellow historical society members that were also part of the Chicago Academy of Sciences. Dr. Raymond Janssen went to Northwestern University, later receiving his master's and Ph.D. from the University of Chicago; in the 1930s he wrote many papers on the Trail Marker Trees in the Chicagoland area as well as many other states.

Frank Grover, Raymond Janssen, Raymond Gloede, and Herbert Mulford, all from Illinois, were four of the leading authorities on Trail Marker Trees in the early 1900's. This helped to make people in Illinois more aware of the Trail Marker Tree systems that existed in the towns along the North Shore suburbs and Chicago stretching up to the Chain O'Lakes region and beyond. The Cub Scouts, Boy Scouts, and Girl Scouts of Illinois were often taken on short trips to learn about the Trail Marker Trees in nearby towns and villages. As a result of these trips some of the scouts would carry on the tradition of caring for and protecting these trees, as well as educating new generations about the importance of the trees. In addition, the Daughters of the American Revolution participated in the locating of mounds and the documenting of old American Indian trails helping the governmental survey groups. Through these efforts they became aware of the Trail Marker Trees and began to locate, document, and photograph these trees.

After living at The Grove, I moved near Half Day, a neighborhood of the village of Vernon Hills, to a home on the Des Plaines River near the Ryerson Conservation Area. This area was known to have been a place of Native American habitation; it was the site of a large Indian village located just off of a main Indian trail. Several years later I moved further northwest to Ackerman Island on the north end of Nippersink Lake, another area known for its Native American history. Years later I once again moved further north and finally settled in the Chain O'Lakes area, near the Wisconsin border.

The boys, Matt and John Downes, camping at Shawano Wisconsin in 1926.

1925 on the Chain O' Lakes, Nick Downes, John Downes, and Matt Downes-Dennis' father and uncles.

Photo taken by John Downes in Africa during WWII. 1943

Kayak built by John Downes Jr. in the 1960's, Dennis used it for water travels for 20 years and then mounted it pointing due north as his very own marker.

Matt Downes (Dennis' father) on his motorcycle, an Indian, in Mountain Home, Idaho. 1945

Nick Downes (Dennis' uncle) in the late 1930's.

The first bronze Trail Marker Tree sculpture, cast by Harry Spell of Art Casting of Illinois in 1995. Behind the sculpture, the original painting *Heading North* can be seen. This painting is based on a Trail Marker Tree system in Wisconsin. Photo taken during an exhibit at The Grove Redfield Center.

Here I have continued my interest and research on the Indians of the Great Lakes Region and beyond. At this point the Trail Marker Trees became more than just a topic of interest; I began studying and researching the trees everywhere I went.

The concept of the Trail Marker Tree system became even clearer for me when I first saw one of Janssen's papers in which he explained what he had learned about the Trail Marker Trees from predecessors who were members of the Chicago Academy of Sciences. I found this paper through the use of the Interlibrary Loan System; I was able to access and receive books and articles from across the country. I then made the decision go to every state where Dr. Raymond Janssen and Dr. Frank Grover had documented Trail Marker Trees. Little did I know then, the Trail Marker Trees would change the direction of my life.

During the course of my study I also located a number of ancient Indian artifacts that I brought to the Milwaukee Museum to have verified. In the early 90s, the head of the Ethnology Department at the Milwaukee Museum, Ann McMullen, was kind enough to show me artifacts that were not on display for the general public to see; in fact, only some of what is stored in museums actually becomes part of formal exhibits and displays. I was able to see collections of Native American symbolism, much of which was from the Great Lakes Region. We also discussed my study on the Trail Marker Trees, and McMullen helped to guide me to new sources of information on the subject that also helped to

further my study. Ann McMullen now works for the Smithsonian National Museum of the Native American.

I feel it was the combination of my early experiences and love of the outdoors that drove me to travel well over 100,000 miles, visiting over 40 states and all of the bordering Canadian provinces over the three decades of this study. During this time I slept mostly in my Ford pickup trucks; I installed screens into the cap in the bed of the truck for the summer and extra insulation on the floor for the winter. I spent my time talking to local historians, arborists, loggers, ethnologists, foresters, archeologists, DNR personnel, anthropologists, American Indians, Native American historical experts, and other Trail Marker Tree enthusiasts. I have given lectures and distributed papers that I have written about the Trail Marker Trees at over 125 shows and exhibits across the United States and abroad over the past three decades.

One particular 60-day exhibit at the Lake County Discovery Museum brought in over 3,000 guests in 2002. I underestimated the impact that these early lectures and exhibits would have, but it was clear to see when many interest groups and websites later sprang up on the internet. My Uncle John said that there is no substitute for field research; I was planting the seeds and I would see the benefit in years to come. He was right; years later people who had heard my lectures or met me during research trips to their area began contacting me with examples and locations of many Trail Marker Trees that had not yet been documented. To this day I still receive photographs, phone calls, and emails as a result of these early personal connections. These contacts have helped to increase the scope of my study beyond what I could have ever imagined.

My goal throughout this study has always been to give credit to those that have come before me, those that helped to document, photograph, and record the importance of these Native American icons from centuries ago. As I became aware that these ancient markers were being damaged and quickly disappearing, even since the beginning of my study, my goal became to ensure that these trees are protected and never forgotten. I began shaping these trees over 20 years ago so that new Trail Marker Trees can begin to replace those that have been lost, more recently I have shaped trees in cooperation with forest services and the DNR. I have planted and shaped numerous trees in historically significant locations and along ancient trails like the Green Bay Trail in both Illinois and Wisconsin. I have also involved my artistic talents in sketching, painting, and sculpting to honor these historic icons. Some of these works on are permanent display at museums, public libraries, historical societies, national landmarks, and private collections nationwide. Over the years I have created life-like and life-size sculptures of the Trail Marker Trees, as well as smaller bronze representations to serve as permanent reminders of these historical landmarks.

Dennis studying buffalo jumps and trails in Montana in the late 1980s.

Luis and Harold Downes, 1954, on Cedar Island, Chain O'Lakes.

Bill Ostman, Dennis Downes, Jim Siano, Peter Quinn, and Tom English heading to the Garden of the Gods in Dennis' Landcruiser Jeep. 1972

Functional igloo made by Dennis, Patrick, Harold, Luis, and Dennis' friend Mark Mitchem, no parents involved. Photo taken by Shirley Mitchem. 1961

The Grove Store
THE GROVE
A National Historic Landmark
Kennicott House-Redfield Ce
Interpretive Center
Glenview Park District 1421 Milwauke
Art
DENNIS

Dennis, years later after living there, standing outside The Grove. Now he has a yearly show and Trail Tree exhibit at The Grove.

Robert Kennicott, explorer and scientist, lived at The Grove

Chapter One

DEFINING THE TRAIL MARKER TREES AND THEIR IMPORTANCE

Before paved roads, street signs, railroads, and road maps, even our noted heroes of exploration and Native Americans have admitted to being lost. Without a system to help travelers find their way, navigating through the Americas years ago could prove very difficult. The Native Americans created a navigational system of their own to aid them in their travels. The Trail Marker Trees, as well as Marker Trees in general, were part of an extensive land and water navigation system in our country that already was in place long before the arrival of the first European settlers.

While the Native Americans had many trails in place, both their own foot paths and the extensive buffalo traces (well-worn trails throughout the country made from the migration patterns of the buffalo herds); the Trail Marker Trees served as exit signs off of these routes bringing them to areas of specific interest, much like exit signs off of our major highways and interstates today. These Trail Marker Trees would have had to be distinctively different in their shape than simply a tree that had been deformed by nature. One type of Trail Marker Tree was the Directional Trail Marker Tree which was bent in an arch approximately three to four feet off the ground with one single upright limb; the arch of the tree pointing in the direction the Native Americans were supposed to follow. The Directional Trees could guide the traveler from one tree to the next until their destination was finally reached. Some of these trees would have guided the traveler to fresh water springs, exposed stone deposits, areas where specific plants could be gathered, ceremonial sites, areas of portage, and other specific areas of significance. The widespread trails created by animal migration that they followed never would have taken them to these many specific sites of human interest and necessity.

This study does not focus on one particular American Indian tribe; rather it encompasses a majority of the North American tribes. The majority of tribes would have used the Trail Marker Tree system or a variation of it to navigate their complex forest systems, vast plains, and water ways. Other forms of navigational aids were used throughout North America, such as standing stones, stone cairns, petroglyphs, pictographs, arborglyphs, and even the placement of stones in trees. However, it is well documented that the majority of Native American tribes used trees to aid them in their travels.

While there would be ample sources of water along the migration trails that would meet the needs of the animals, the Native Americans preferred to drink from only fresh water sources. Fresh water springs would be free from the water born diseases found in stagnant water and other water sources. The fresh water springs only occur sporadically, while some were easily located others were very difficult to find. Having the Directional Marker Trees to guide them to the springs that were more difficult to find would be a great advantage on long journeys; it would save them time and ensure access to fresh water.

Just as the migration trails would not lead the Native Americans directly to the fresh water springs, the trails also would not lead them to the exposed stone and mineral deposits.

The Native Americans needed stones and minerals that had vitreous (glass-like) qualities like chert, flint, jasper, obsidian, and chalcedony, to name a few. They would also need stones with qualities of strength, coarseness, and permanence, such as granite and basalt. These stones and minerals were needed to make a wide variety of stone tools, weapons, and adornments necessary to their way of life. The stones and minerals that had these specific qualities would be available to them only in certain areas as exposed deposits. Some of these deposits could be easily found on the shores of many of the Great

page 23
Directional quill burst by author

This drawing by the author depicts the Directional Trail Marker Tree.

All of these pieces are examples of the many different kinds of stones and minerals the Native Americans would use for their tools and ceremonial pieces. All of the artifacts shown here are from the Dennis' personal and documented collection.

This rare ceremonial scorpion piece was found in Oklahoma, near a river bed by Native American Historical Expert, Steve Young. This is the first time it has ever been seen in a book.

One piece from Dennis' collection, a Madison Side Notched variant (Osceola) that is 3,000-4,000 years old. Documented by the Milwaukee Museum.

A rare carving from the false face society, this piece was used in healing ceremonies. Shown to Dennis by Steve Young.

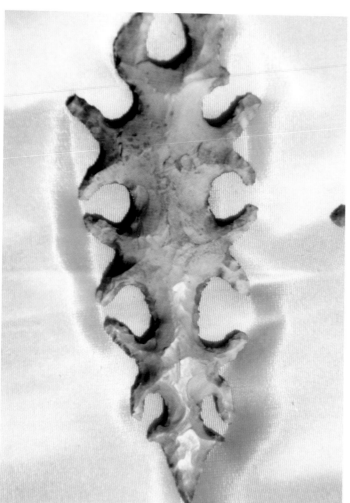

Lakes and rivers, but deposits inland were often in remote areas. A number of these deposit areas would become recognized later as chipping stations because of all the remnants of stone flakes left behind from the Native Americans working on their tools, weapons, and adornments. The Native Americans would mark these more difficult locations using the Trail Marker Trees. The Marker Trees were also used to direct the Native Americans to the exposed copper and lead deposits, materials that were also used for their practical and ornamental properties.

An important resource the Native Americans would have been able to utilize were the caves and cave systems in certain areas of North America. Trail Marker Trees would have been used to guide the Native Americans on a direct route to these often obscure caves. The caves supplied many advantages to the traveler; the ability to store caches such as dried food goods and weapons, as well as supplying a safe shelter from bad weather or hostile enemies. The traveler, having the advantage of the Trail Marker Tree to guide him to the general area of the cave, would be able to disguise the cave by covering it with brush, so only he would be able to locate it. Larger caves would be used for ceremonial purposes and could provide shelter as well.

Other necessities to the Native American way of life included special plants used for medicinal purposes and plants used for dyes, stains, and paints that were integral to their ceremonies and adornments. Plants such as bloodroot, motherwort, and yarrow were used for their medicinal qualities; where as, plants such as pokeweed and dogwood were used for

A rare spear point and effigy pieces, part of Steve Young's collection.

The author creating some of his own natural dyes and paints, similar to what the Native Americans would have used centuries ago.

This drawing depicts a special form of grafted tree, most often used to indicate portage. Drawing submitted by Paul O'Hara

dyes, just to name a few. Areas where these plants grew in abundance could be marked because of their importance. Other areas of great importance such as ceremonial sites, medicine wheels, and ancient earth works may be marked as well. Along with marking the paths to areas of important plants that would need to be gathered, the trees would also guide the Native Americans to areas of good hunting and good fishing. Their culture was largely based on hunting and gathering and knowing areas were these tasks could be completed more efficiently would be essential to survival.

One of the greatest purposes the Trail Marker Trees served was to mark areas of safe crossing across rivers. The need to keep not only themselves, but their goods and belongings dry was of the highest importance. During a long journey, the Native Americans could not afford to have all of their supplies, including food, clothing, and plant materials, become wet and damaged. Thus, they would need to cross the rivers in areas where the river was shallow enough to keep their supplies dry; these areas were referred to as fords by the European settlers. The Directional Trail Marker Trees would guide the Native Americans to these fords.

Trail Marker Trees were also used to indicate locations of portage along a river. During travel by water, the American Indians would have to know where to leave the body of water they were on to avoid obstacles such as rapids and waterfalls or to begin travel by a land trail. Another type of tree used to indicate portage or locations to depart from the rivers were

grafted trees. Grafted trees are two trees that were grown together to form an arch with one upright limb or an "H" pattern. Both the Markers Trees and the grafted trees would be easily seen from the river and could also be used to indicate which branch of the river to follow. Helen Hornbeck Tanner, the nation's foremost researcher and disseminator of Native American history of the Great Lakes Region, has confirmed the use of these grafted trees, as well as the Trail Marker Tree system in general, during a recent interview with the author.

Another purpose the Trail Marker Trees served was to designate boundaries between tribal territories. It was important for the Native Americans to know when they were leaving their tribe's territory and entering into another territory, as this could have dire consequences. Trail Marker Trees for this purpose varied greatly from region to region and tribe to tribe.

The Native American way of life, like so many other cultures, occasionally involved disputes with neighboring tribes. These disputes could be settled swiftly or could last for decades. As a result, certain travel routes would be restricted during these times of conflict. When the conflicts ended and normal travel patterns could resume, many of their secondary trails would be overgrown and difficult to recognize. However, if the trail had been marked by Trail Marker Trees, the path could be relocated and reestablished with minimal effort.

Trail Marker Trees would be particularly important to certain areas of the country that were lacking obvious landmarks and that experienced extended periods of cloud cover. Landmarks like the natural rock outcroppings that would appear above the tree line, mountains, and plateaus that travelers could use as a reference from miles away were not available in certain areas. Also, certain parts of the country are prone to heavier cloud cover year round. This cloud cover would prevent the traveler from relying on the sun and stars to determine his location and guide his navigation; whereas, in other areas of the country the sun and stars could almost always be used as a reference for the traveler. Conditions like these would make the Trail Marker Tree a much needed navigational aid.

Throughout the country there are many variances in the shape and style of these culturally altered trees. Although the Trail Marker Trees varied, it would always be clear that these trees had been shaped by man and not by nature, in order for this system to work efficiently. Just as the shapes and styles of the trees vary; the names for the trees also vary. The trees have been called witness trees, water trees, thong trees, chair trees, signal trees, and language trees. For the purpose of this study, the trees will be referred to by the terms Trail Marker Tree and Marker Tree as this has been how the trees have been referred to in literature, signs, and plaques going back over a century. However, what the trees are called is not nearly as important as understanding their purpose and that was to mark the trails. Today these ancient symbols from the past are all too quickly disappearing from our landscape. The need for the trees slowly began to decline as the new 'American' culture began to take over. The Native Americans began trading with the settlers and could obtain food supplies, medicine, and manufactured tools and weapons. Soon after the Native Americans would become relocated onto reservations and the Trail Marker Trees would no longer have a purpose, nor would they be replaced. These culturally altered living artifacts that remain should be treated with reverence and respect.

This study has been based on three decades of field research combined with researching hundreds of books, writings, maps, and surveys from the 17th century to present day, and numerous personal interviews with historical experts from across the country. This study is by far the most inclusive study of the Trail Marker Trees to date and the author intends to continue this study well into the future.

Chapter Two

SHAPING THE TRAIL MARKER TREES

The Trail Marker Trees' distinctive shapes, that separated them from naturally occurring deformities, were achieved by several specific techniques. These techniques varied from tribe to tribe and from region to region due to differing cultural aspects and soil conditions. Trees chosen to become Trail Marker Trees needed to possess certain qualities. The American Indians knew the qualities and traits of the different species of trees in North America, as the trees were an essential part of their everyday life.

Trail Marker Trees were usually selected from the hardwood families for their flexibility while young, followed by their permanence and ability to retain their shape well into the future. In the Great Lakes Region, oaks were typically chosen to be used as Trail Marker Trees. Following is a detailed example of one specific shaping technique with detailed sketches drawn by the author.

The young sapling would be shaped when it was approximately an inch and a half in diameter and roughly eight to ten feet in height. Based on needs and availability, they could use larger or smaller saplings. This young sapling would be bent in the desired direction of the trail to be taken; the bend would be approximately three to four feet off the ground. The sapling would be tied to a stake that would be driven into the ground, or if rockier soil conditions existed, it would simply be tied to a substantial boulder, serving the same purpose (Refer to Sketch I). Once the tree was secured, it was simply left alone for the next year. The next to play a role in shaping the Trail Marker Tree would be Mother Nature; she would soon send a row of buds popping up all along the arch that has been formed by bending and staking the small sapling (Refer to Sketch II).

The following year, when the Native American would pass by the tree, he would leave the buds on the top and center of the arch alone and remove all other buds. He would also ensure that the buckskin tie and stake were in good condition and continue on his way (Refer to Sketch III). Over the next few years, the buds that the American Indian had left on the top of the arch will have started shooting skyward. At this point the shaper would select one, two, or three of these new branches to allow to continue growing (depending on the type of Trail Marker Tree being formed) and remove the rest and again go on his way (Refer to Sketch IV).

The Native American having decided to make this tree a Directional Trail Marker Tree would then remove all but one of the skyward branches. The single branch that was left shooting skyward would soon become the new trunk of the tree, giving the Trail Marker Tree one of its distinct characteristics (Refer to Sketch V). If two upright branches pointing skyward were left, these branches would need to be spaced far enough apart to allow for future growth of each branch. These two branches would later become the main trunks of this Trail Marker Tree (Refer to Sketch VII). This kind of Trail Marker Tree is most often referred to as a double trunk Trail Marker Tree. Similarly, three evenly spaced upright branches could be left to become a triple trunk Trail Marker Tree.

During the next few years, the shaper will inspect the tree only in passing. When the Native American decides the tree is ready, he will perform the final step in shaping the Trail Marker Tree. The final step is to remove the old section of the arched trunk that extends past the new skyward

Sketch I

3'

Sketch II

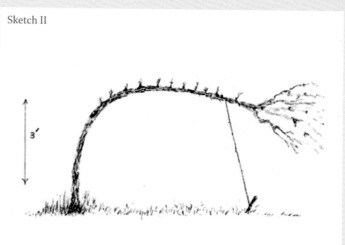

3'

Sketch III

3'

Sketch IV

3'

This young tree is being shaped as a Trail Marker Tree along the ancient Green Bay Trail. This tree is in the early stages, where numerous buds are springing up along the newly arched tree.

This walnut tree is Dennis' first attempt at shaping an example of a boundary tree, after seeing the well-known boundary tree in Alabama years ago. Photo taken by Liz Fox.

Sketch V

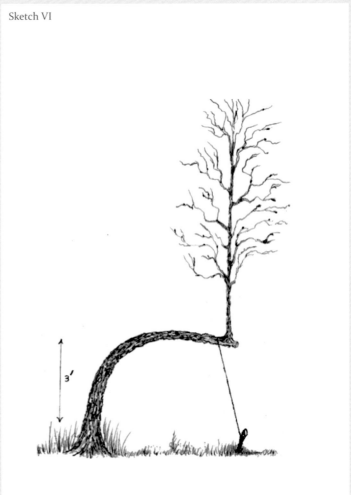

Sketch VI

branch. This process leaves the skyward branch as the new trunk of the tree. This being completed, a new piece of buckskin and a fresh stake may be resecured to the sapling to ensure it keeps its shape in the coming years (Refer to Sketch VI). This step would need to be completed with the single trunk, double trunk, and triple trunk Trail Marker Trees.

This technique is just one of many that have been documented. Variations of this technique can be used to accomplish other shapes and styles, like the special form of Trail Marker Tree described by Raymond Janssen in which the lowermost branch of an older tree is utilized for shaping (Refer to Sketch VIII). Another and more complex variation was formed by grafting two trees together which was a technique passed on generation to generation. In reality, what has amounted to only a few minutes of actual work would ultimately result in a distinctive Trail Marker Tree that would last for centuries to come. After a Trail Marker Tree was shaped to mark a new route, the need to replace it would only come upon the tree's death, giving the Native Americans ample time to select and shape its replacement.

This distinct horizontal shape the Trail Marker Tree has taken on will stand out in a forest of vertical trees. The height of the horizontal portion of the Trail Marker Tree would also approximate the height of some of the wild game the Native Americans would have been trained to spot

in the forest. In a culture based on hunting and gathering, the hunter would be trained from childhood to recognize horizontal shapes in the forest in hopes that it was wild game, which would supply the food so necessary to their existence. This distinctive characteristic would make the Trail Marker Tree easily recognizable to the Native American.

The use of trees for navigational purposes demonstrated how resourceful the Native Americans truly were, as the trees were a plentiful and lasting resource. This system was well thought out as demonstrated by the distinct and purposeful shape of the Trail Marker Trees. The shape itself, was not only made to stand out horizontally in a vertical world at approximately the height of game, but also, the shape would still be visible above the height of the average snow fall in the Great Lakes Region. The subtle variations in the shape of the Trail Marker Trees, specifically the number of upright limbs, would relay information instantly. A single upright trunk would have a different meaning than a double or triple trunk Trail Marker Tree; these shapes and meanings would vary from tribe to tribe.

Throughout this book the author is shown in a number of the photos near the Trail Marker Trees to help provide visual scale to the size of these trees. Dennis has been shaping young Trail Marker and Marker Trees for decades and has included some photographs of these trees as young saplings.

Sketch VII

Sketch VIII

Dennis next to a young bur oak that he began shaping years ago in Illinois. Photo taken by Liz Fox

Dennis checking on the young Trail Marker Tree during a major flood.

The author experimenting with
an alternative method of shaping.
This shaped Trail Maker Tree is
located in Wisconsin. Photo taken
by Brian Buchholz.

This photo, taken in Illinois, shows a young ash being shaped into a double trunk Trail Marker Tree. Photo taken by the author.

Dennis began shaping this directional Trail Maker Tree many years ago, purposefully near an ancient site of Native American inhabitation in Wisconsin. Photo taken by Liz Fox"

Chapter Three

ILLINOIS

The state of Illinois is known as the 'Prairie State,' and in earlier days, its fertile plains supplied an endless amount of grasses for the large buffalo herds that made their migration through the state as well as the large deer and elk herds. During the time of the early settlers, the plains grasses were as tall as the backs of the settlers' horses and described as oceans of grass, extending as far as the eye could see. While the prairies expanded across the central portion of the state, the southern tip and northern region were covered in old-growth forest, forests that had not been disturbed by man, hosting some of the largest trees in the Mississippi Valley. These great trees sparked an interest in the public as well as the scientific community, increasing the studies and awareness not only of the ancient trees, but also of the Trail Marker Trees and Marker Trees in the region.

The Great Lakes Region, particularly the state of Illinois, where the author grew up, has a long history with the Trail Marker Trees. The Trail Marker Trees have been documented in the state going back centuries. Hundreds of years ago, Illinois was part of the Northwest Territory along with five other states; Ohio, Wisconsin, Indiana, Michigan, and Minnesota. Of these states, Illinois was centrally located, rich in game and natural resources, and had an extensive navigable river system as well as access to the Great Lakes. All of these attributes made the area very appealing to both the Native Americans and European fur trappers. The Native American tribes that were in the area throughout the 1600's, 1700's, and early 1800's as documented by Helen Hornbeck Tanner in the "Atlas of the Great Lakes Indian History" are: the Illinois Confederation (Kaskaskia, Cahokia, Peoria, Chinkoa, Coiracoentanon, Espeminkia, Maroa, Matchinkoa, Michibousa, Tamaroa, Moingwena, Michigamea, Albiui, Amonokoa, Chepoussa, Negawichi, and Tapouara), Shawnee, Ottawa, Potawatomi, Sauk, Mesquakie, Tionontati, Miami, Ojibwa, Mascouten, Iowa, Peoria, Kaskaskia, Winnebago, Menominee, Kickapoo, and Piankashaw. Not all of these tribes were in the area simultaneously; throughout the time period the tribes moved in and out of the area as hunting resources and tribal wars dictated.

Many of the European fur trappers, mostly the French as Illinois was controlled by the French Empire until 1763, took Indian wives and, as a result, became more accepted by the Indian tribes than other Europeans. One of the most well-known

page 41
Dennis at the Garden of the
Gods during one of his many visits,
the view from this point shows
the breathtaking beauty of the park.
Photo by Greg Prochnow

A buffalo grazing on the plains.
Photo taken by Dennis.

Map of the "Northwest Territory"

Jean Baptiste Pointe Du Sable,
Bronze. This sculpture was
donated by members of Chicago's
Haitian-American community,
sculptor Erik Blome.

Photo of Gurdon Saltonstall Hubbard

Photo of a watercolor painting by
Mary Martin Engel (of Wilmette)
depicting Antoine Ouilmette's
marriage to Archange

fur traders of the 1700's was a man of African American and
French decent, Jean Baptiste Pointe du Sable; he was declared
the Founder of Chicago by the state of Illinois. Du Sable was
married to a Potawatomi woman (Kittahawa) and was accepted
into her tribe, even becoming a high ranking member of the
tribe and referred to as "Black Chief." Gurdon Saltonstall
Hubbard was another well-known fur trapper. He arrived in the
Chicago area in 1818 as an indentured worker to Astor's American Fur Company. Hubbard came to be well-liked by the Indian
Tribes throughout the area and even became the adopted son
of Chief Waba of the Kickapoo tribe, later marrying one of the
Kankakee Indian women. Hubbard became named "Papa-ma-
ta-be" or "Swift-Walker" by the local Indians after warning a
nearby town of impending danger. He went on to build
Chicago's first stockyard and to be a leading figure in the fur
trading industry. Another prominent fur trapper and trader in
the 1800's was Antoine Ouilmette, a French-Canadian, after
whom the Chicago suburb of Wilmette was named. Ouilmette
and his family had land near Hubbard and were very close with
the area tribes; he married Archange Marie Chevalier, a
French-Potawatomi woman. Upon Ouilmette's land was where
many of the first documented Trail Marker Trees were located;
his land covered what is now known as the Wilmette and
Winnetka areas. The tribes were more willing to share knowledge
with these fur trappers about areas of good hunting and trapping, techniques used to mark trails, and other valuable information. Later this information would be passed on both to the

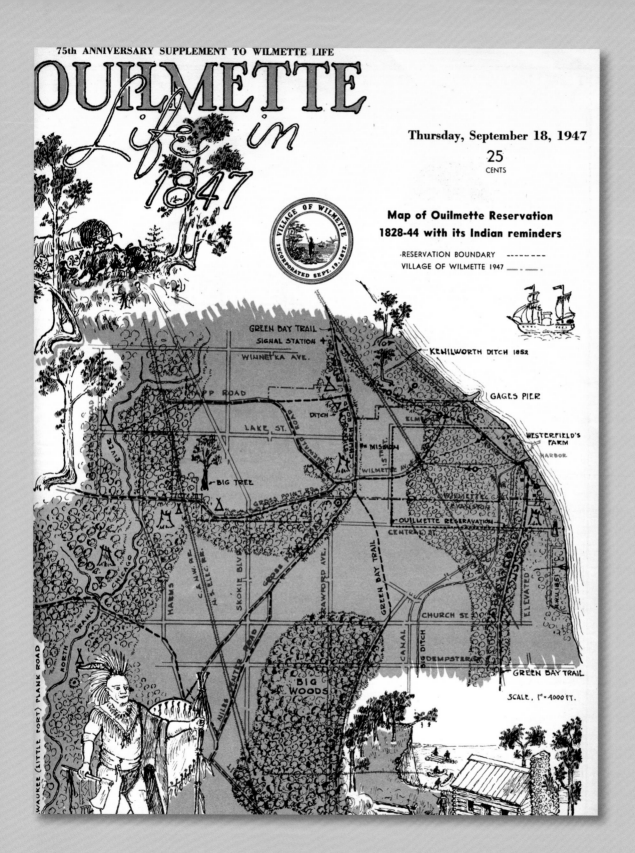

75th ANNIVERSARY SUPPLEMENT TO WILMETTE LIFE

OUILMETTE Life in 1847

Thursday, September 18, 1947

25
CENTS

**Map of Ouilmette Reservation
1828-44 with its Indian reminders**

RESERVATION BOUNDARY - - - - - - - -
VILLAGE OF WILMETTE 1947 —·—·—·—

VILLAGE OF WILMETTE · INCORPORATED SEPT. 19, 1872.

GREEN BAY TRAIL
SIGNAL STATION
WINNETKA AVE.
KENILWORTH DITCH 1852
GAGES PIER
APP ROAD
DITCH
WESTERFIELD'S FARM
LAKE ST.
HARBOR
ELM
MISSION
BIG TREE
WILMETTE
WILMETTE EVANSTON
OUILMETTE RESERVATION
CENTRAL ST.
RIVER
CHICAGO
HARMS
SKOKIE RIVER
CROSS POINT
CRAWFORD AVE.
GREEN BAY TRAIL
ELEVATED
CHURCH ST.
NORTH BRANCH
MILWAUKEE (LITTLE FORT) PLANK ROAD
BIG WOODS
CANAL
BIG DITCH
DEMPSTER ST.
GREEN BAY TRAIL

SCALE, 1" = 1000 FT.

Historical map by Charles Henderson, showing trail tree locations, on the cover of the special supplement of *Wilmette Life* for September 18, 1947, published to celebrate the village's 75th anniversary. Photograph courtesy of the Wilmette Historical Museum provided by Patrick Leary Ph.D., Curator who worked personally with the author.

Byron Schrock standing next to Dennis on this old-growth sycamore marker tree, contacted Mr. Downes in regards to this tree after seeing his 2003 Trail Marker Tree Exhibit and

16' Sculpture at the Wildlife Prairie State Park. Mr. Schrock's grandfather had been told by the local Indians that the large limb of this tree pointed towards a local river. This tree is estimated to be over 400 years old and has become a local landmark in Peoria.

Dennis in front of an old-growth bur oak still standing in southern Illinois, estimated to be at least 500 years old. He has documented several other old-growth trees throughout Illinois that are still standing. Photo taken by Greg Prochnow.

missionaries and the early settlers. This same scenario was common in other areas of the country known for trapping, but this area was fortunate to have some of the most extensive early documentation. As a result, many of the fur trappers that were aware of the Trail Marker Trees and their uses later passed this information on to the missionaries and early settlers.

As this information was passed on from generation to generation, certain individuals and groups went out of their way to start documenting the concept of Trail Marker Trees in order to give honor and credit to this Native American form of land navigation. The immense interest in the old-growth forests drew many botanists and dendrologists from abroad to this area, while studying the old-growth trees they often came across Trail Marker Trees. As time went on, more people became aware of these trees and began their own documentation and photographic studies. Some of the most well-known advocates of the Trail Marker Trees in this area were: the Chicago Academy of Sciences, landscape architects, local historians and historical societies, the National Society of the Daughters of the American Revolution (D.A.R.), Boy Scouts of America, Girl Scouts of America, Garden Clubs, Arboretums, and forestry departments. One of the earliest and most in-depth photographic studies was completed by Bess Bower-Dunn, a Waukegan historian; her study began in 1912. The D.A.R. also known for some of the earliest photographic documentation of the trees, as well as placing bronze tablets near the Trail Marker Trees that explained their significance

and credited the Native Americans. The D.A.R. even coordinated special ceremonies that took place at the Trail Marker Trees, inviting Native Americans to return to the area and participate in these naming ceremonies. One local member of the D.A.R., Mrs. Ickes, gave the address for one such ceremony where the Trail Marker Tree system was explained to the audience and a Trail Marker Tree in Glencoe was commemorated with a bronze tablet that was inscribed:

"This Indian Trail Tree Marked a New Pathway Thru the Forest, the Hunting Ground of the Indian Tribes, Along the Shores of Lake Michigan. Tablet Placed by the Glencoe Chapter, Daughters of the American Revolution 1928"

Throughout just the North Shore area, the D.A.R. placed numerous bronze tablets commemorating these culturally altered living artifacts, some dating as early as 1911.

Not only were the Trail Marker Trees in this area recognized and commemorated by individuals and groups, they were also referred to in many early publications. The Lake County Book of Records at the Recorder's Office holds a survey from 1852 that has a sketch of a Trail Marker Tree completed by an official Lake County Surveyor, Mr. Hale. In 1912, John Halsey, LL.D. of Lake Forest College, talks about two notable Trail Marker Trees in Lake County in his book *"A History of Lake County Illinois."* Halsey also discusses two ancient cottonwood marker trees; one a great cottonwood tree,

This photograph was taken by Bess Dunn in 1912. This Trail Marker Tree was located in Lake Forest Illinois. Photograph courtesy of the Lake County Museum, Lakewood Forest Preserve.

This photo depicts the monument of a triple trunk Trail Marker Tree that was known to point to the largest Native American village in the Evanston area. When the tree was still living, it stood at the entrance to the Cavalry Cemetery along the train tracks. Out of respect for the tree and the Native Americans, the Daughters of the American Revolution, with the help of the Evanston Historical Society, had the tree turned to a monument and placed at the Davis Street Park. The D.A.R. also had a bronze tablet placed near the tree that was inscribed *"This Red Oak was a Pottawatomie Trail Tree which grew on Green Bay Trail immediately west of Cavalry Station where it pointed to a large Indian village located on and east of the site of Bowmanville."*

This is a photograph of Bess Dunn standing in the bend of a known type of Marker Tree in Lake Bluff, referred to by Raymond Janssen. Although this was not a traditional Trail Marker Tree, there were two known trees shaped in this fashion. Photo courtesy of the Lake County Museum, Lakewood Forest Preserve.

pages 48–49
In April 1928, the Daughters of the American Revolution hosted a ceremony honoring a Glencoe Indian Trail Marker Tree. This ceremony included the involvement of Chief Evergreen and two other Indian men. Many local boy scouts were also able to attend. Mrs. Anna Ickes, wife of Harold Ickes, the Secretary of the Department of Interior, helped to organize this ceremony and spoke as part of the event.

located on the southern edge of the Onwentsia Club. Fortu-
nately, golf courses became sanctuaries for these Marker and
Trail Marker Trees, saving them from the loggers, saw. These
trees were a welcome addition to the landscape, and these
ancient landmarks became a point of conversation at the many
private and public golf courses. The other great Marker Tree
was located on the edge of a road leading from Glencoe to
Shermerville (now known as Northbrook). Another ancient
cottonwood Marker Tree known to have been located on the
Kloepfer Farm just outside of Wilmette was written about by
Jens Jensen, a renowned landscape architect, in a 1915 volume
of *"American Forestry."* This giant cottonwood was over 600
years old at the time of its demise and was known as the Black
Hawk or Potawatomi Tree throughout history. In 1922, K.S.
Nicholson wrote *"Historic American Trees"* and discussed the
well-known line of 11 white oak Trail Marker Trees that stood
in perfect alignment and led from Highland Park around the
marshes to another Indian village. She also mentions another
line of white elms near Evanston that lead towards Lake
Michigan. In 1934, Raymond Janssen, botanist, wrote an article,
"Indian Trail Trees," for the American Forestry Association
that refers to one of the dedications by the Daughters of
the American Revolution in Evanston. Mr. Horton wrote a
10 page paper entitled, *Indian Trail Trees in Lake County*
in 1935, describing not only the location of many Trail Marker
Trees but also their importance. Even the United States
Department of Agriculture used an Illinois Trail Marker Tree

This photo, taken by Hazel Avery, shows a Highland Park Trail Marker Tree that stood at the Exmoor Country Club, 1957.

An article about a Cook County Indian Trail Tree from the *Daily News Chicago*, June 23, 1920.

A REMINDER OF OLD INDIAN DAYS.

TREE ON FOREST PRESERVE IN PALOS TOWNSHIP WHICH ONCE SERVED AS GUIDE POST FOR RED MEN, HISTORIANS SAY.

[By a staff photographer of The Daily News.]

ON land recently acquired by the Cook county forest preserve in Palos township stands a freak tree, beloved of school children in the neighborhood. Old settlers remember it as the "Indian tree." According to researches of Frank R. Grover in possession of the Chicago Historical society there are eleven such trees in this section of the state. The theory is that Indian hunters in the early days bent over young trees for guide posts. The tree in Palos township stands on land formerly owned by Former Chief of Police Francis O'Neil.

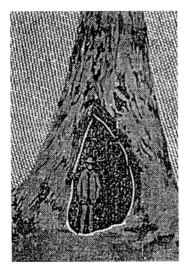

This is the photograph that accompanied a 1901 article in the *Chicago Tribune* titled, "Great Tree with a Remarkable History." Although the photo quality prevents its viewer from seeing, behind the man in the photograph there are three horses inside the opening in the tree. Photograph courtesy of the Wilmette Historical Museum

Raymond Gloede took this photo of the Potawatomi tree in 1903 before they moved it to the Gloede Nursery. Photo courtesy of *Roots, A Glenview Story* and the Glenview Historical Society.

Wilmette ladies on an afternoon bicycle outing to the Potawatomi Tree on Glenview Road in 1897. Photograph courtesy of the Wilmette Historical Museum

as their example describing the trees in *Trees: Yearbook of Agriculture*, published in 1949. The Wisconsin Archeologist is the longest continuously published archeological journal in North America; they published articles about the Trail Marker Trees in 1940 and 1965, including examples of trees from Illinois. Also in 1940, *National History Magazine* published an article referring to the Trail Marker Trees of this area. *The World Book Encyclopedia*, 1955, uses an example of an Illinois tree to depict an Indian Trail Marker Tree. Even the famous *Life Magazine* referred to the Illinois (Highland Park and Evanston) Indian Trail Trees, when doing a piece on Historic Trees in 1962. A more recent publication, This Land of Lakes and Rivers an Illustrated History of Lake County, by Virginia Mullery in 1989, included a photograph (taken in 1957 by Hazel Avery member of the Bannockburn Garden Club) of an Indian Trail Tree that stood at the Exmoor Country Club in Highland Park. This tree was commemorated with a bronze tablet permanently mounted on a boulder, placed by the Daughters of the American Revolution. This boulder is all that is left to mark the location of this tree as it has since perished.

It is obvious that the state of Illinois has been very involved in recognizing and documenting the Trail Marker Trees in the past. During the past three decades, the author has received support from many current groups and individuals that have greatly aided his study. Dennis would like to acknowledge: Dr. Harry Spell, historian and foundry owner; Knonozo, Potawatomi historical expert in northeastern Illinois and southeastern Wisconsin; Terrence R. Lyons, attorney and historian; Judy Hughes, president of the Northbrook Historical Society and chairman of the Northbrook Arts Commission; Janet Gallimore, former executive director of the Lake County Discovery Museum in Wauconda, currently the executive director of the Idaho State Historical Society; Michael Griem of the Exmoor Country Club; Amy Blue, head of the Reference Department at the Antioch Public Library, Arthur Landwehr, Project Manager; Roger Shule, President of the Antioch Fine Arts Foundation; Patti Van Cleave, executive director of the Winnetka Historical Society; Patrick Leary, Curator, Kathy Hussey-Arnston, executive director of the Wilmette Historical Museum; Brian Buchholz, arborist and employee of the Lake County Forest Preserve District; Nadean Buchholz, horticulturist; Greg and Ann Prochnow, for photography and research; Helen Hornbeck Tanner, author and lecturer at The Newberry Library, Chicago; and Steve Swanson, director and Carol Di Lorenzo, coordinator of the Grove National Historic Landmark and Redfield Estate, Glenview for their ongoing support and assistance. Throughout this chapter their contributions will be recognized through events, photographs, articles, and interviews.

The Potawatomi Tree (also known as the Black Hawk Tree)

This great tree was a landmark of enormous proportion. It was located near the border of Wilmette and Glenview, originally on the Kloepfer Farm property. This Marker Tree was renowned for its size and stature. The tree was used and recognized as a

landmark among pioneers, frontier men, Native Americans, and explorers. According to Jens Jensen, "Black Hawk himself often assembled the chiefs of his confederates around the tree, and many of the campaigns against the white were planned beneath its shadow." According to a *Chicago Tribune*, article written in 1901 (courtesy of the Wilmette Historical Museum), this was probably the largest tree in the United States with the exception of the redwoods in California. The Potawatomi tree was estimated by an English forester, in the 1890s, to be over 600 years old. The tree was over 130 feet tall and a had a large opening that led into an 'apartment' that was over 20 feet high, and nearly 12 feet by 13 feet. When the photograph for the *Chicago Tribune* article was taken, there were three horses standing inside the hollowed out portion of the trunk. Within 40 years prior to the *Chicago Tribune* article, only one limb had fallen from the tree. This single limb provided the farmer that owned the land on which the tree stood with enough firewood for the entire winter. Jens Jensen also documented that this Potawatomi Tree was the only tree in the region that was left unharmed in the great fire of 1832. After the tree had died, in 1903, Mr. Raymond Gloede, a nursery owner, Trail Marker Tree advocate, photographer, and son of Richard Gloede, a landscape architect that helped design Indian Boundary Park, had the hollowed out trunk transported to the Gloede Nursery in Evanston so it could remain a landmark for many years to come. "Among a great many trees of historic value in Illinois the old Black Hawk Tree was the foremost of all," Jens Jensen said in 1915.

Wilmette, Winnetka, and Kenilworth Areas

This area of the North Shore is not only considered one of the most beautiful areas by its current residents, the Indian name of Winnetka in the Algonquin language means "beautiful place;" the area just south, including Wilmette and Kenilworth are equally beautiful. These towns are located along the famous Green Bay Trail that connected Chicago to Green Bay. The Green Bay Trail was not the only trail that passed through the area. In fact, this area had numerous trails. *The History of Lake County*, 1929, says "...this wonderful land at the southern tip of Lake Michigan has been the cross roads of the western continent. Long before the first white man came it was criss-crossed by countless trails of the red men—trails coming up from the south, and the west, and the east, crossed by other trails leading around the foot of the lake..." In an area where so many trails were present, the need to differentiate one trail from another was even more critical. The North Shore area's Trail Marker Tree system helped the Native Americans do just that. Different species of trees were used to mark different trails in order to avoid any confusion. Frank Grover pointed out two clear examples of this including a trail guided by white oak Trail Marker Trees and a trail guided by white elm Trail Marker Trees. Potawatomi historical expert, Knonozo, confirmed this theory during an interview with the author and added his knowledge of a trail guided by red oak Trail Marker Trees that he saw as a younger man, Knonozo is now in his late 70s. With so many Trail Marker Trees, it is no wonder the impact

This photo shows renowned landscape architect Richard Gloede standing beneath the Fuller Lane Trail Marker Tree. The photograph was actually taken by his son, Raymond Gloede. Both father and son were known Trail Marker Tree advocates and Raymond photographed not only local trees, but traveled to other midwestern states to document the trees. Photo courtesy of the Winnetka Historical Society.

This photo is the earliest known photograph of what would later be known as the Fuller Lane tree. It was located across from the cabin built by Simon Doyle in 1836, which was the site of Winnetka's first wedding between Antoine Ouilmette's daughter Elizabeth and Michael Welch. Photo courtesy of Patti Van Cleave, the executive director of the Winnetka Historical Society.

This photo was taken by B. Pines in 1984, shortly before the tree's demise. The plaque that was placed by the Winnetka Historical Society can be clearly seen in this photo. Photo courtesy of Patti Van Cleave, the executive director of the Winnetka Historical Society.

INDIAN TRAIL TREE
THIS ANCIENT WHITE OAK, ONE OF MANY ORIGINALLY FOUND ON THE NORTH SHORE, WAS PRESUMABLY BENT BY THE INDIANS ABOUT 1700, MARKING A TRAIL TO LAKE MICHIGAN

Fuller Lane Winnetka   *Feb 1939*

Fuller Lane trail tree, 1939. Photo by Harriet Joy Scheidenhelm." Photo courtesy of the Wilmette Historical Museum.

Herbert Mulford, author and historian, speaks at the unveiling of a plaque to mark the trail tree at 10th and Greenwood, Wilmette in 1949. Photo courtesy of Patrick Leary of the Wilmette Historical Museum.

David Allen, member of the Wilmette Historical Commission, head of the project honoring two of the Wilmette Trail Marker Trees, holds one of the bronze markers that would be placed by the Greenwood Avenue tree. Photo from an article, courtesy of the Wilmette Historical Museum.

This is a photo of the sign in front of the Wilmette Historical Museum.

of the trees would be great in this area. This area has gone to great lengths to preserve and honor this part of Native American culture in plaques, maps, articles, ceremonies, and books.

The Fuller Lane Tree

The Fuller Lane Trail Marker Tree in Winnetka was one of the oldest and most documented Trail Marker Trees in the area. This tree was commemorated with a bronze plaque that was inscribed, *"Indian Trail Tree; This ancient white oak, one of many originally found on the North Shore, was presumably bent by the Indians about 1700, marking a trail to Lake Michigan."* Author James Pomerantz informed Downes about a restaurant in Winnetka that honored the famous Fuller Lane Tree. The restaurant was named "The Indian Trail" and the Fuller Lane Tree was their inspiration.

The Canterbury Court and Greenwood Avenue Trail Marker Trees

These two Trail Marker Trees once stood in the town of Wilmette and were commemorated by matching bronze plaques, placed by the Wilmette Historical Commission in 1949. These trees were officially designated as Trail Trees by the Wilmette Historical Commission. Associate member of the commission, David Allen, was in charge of this project, honoring these historical landmarks. Herbert Mulford, a noted authority on Wilmette history and author of *Wilmette and the Suburban Whirl: A Sequel to "Frontiers of Old Wilmette,"* (1955) was responsible for much of the research behind this project

and also spoke at the dedication for the trees, addressing the significance of the Indian Trail Marker Trees.

The Greenwood Avenue Trail Marker Tree was a famed tree in its time. This tree was seen in the newspapers, on postcards, and was the subject of a famed artist. Years after the special dedication to this tree and the other nearby Trail Marker Tree on Canterbury Court, the Greenwood Avenue tree was ailing in the late fifties and early sixties. The village of Wilmette decided to fund some 'medical care' to help prolong the life of one of their village's oldest residents-the Trail Marker Tree. In addition to the money spent by the village, in 1965, the president of the Wilmette Historical Society, James Williams, spent some of his own funds to care for the tree as well.

The nearby Canterbury Avenue tree was also commemorated by the village of Wilmette. The bronze plaque placed by the commission still remains today. The first time this tree was brought to the author's attention was by John S. Clark Jr. of the North Shore, a developer and real estate broker, whose family had been in the area for over a century. In the 1980s, Mr. Clark contacted Dennis about many Trail Marker Trees throughout the Illinois and Wisconsin area. Many years later, during a four-month Trail Marker Tree exhibit presented by the author in the Northbrook Historical Museum, Susan Macon saw a photograph of the plaque placed near the Canterbury Avenue tree. Susan informed Dennis that this tree stood in front of her mother's home and later sent him a photograph of her mother and father standing on the Trail Marker Tree.

Photograph of Winnetka author, James Pomerantz, with Downes in Nevada at the PBR Championships for Pomerantz's book signing.

Photo of Patrick Leary, curator of the Wilmette Historical Museum, with Mr. Downes. Mr. Leary was instrumental in helping Mr. Downes locate many old photographs and articles relating to many of the area Trail Marker and Marker Trees.

Photo of a 1939 post card, the text on the back side stated, "Indian trail tree, northeast corner of Greenwood Avenue and 10th Street, Wilmette, Illinois, 1939. Native Americans bent saplings to create such trees to mark a trail or other site." Photograph courtesy of the Wilmette Historical Museum.

This is one of the bronze plaques made by the Wilmette Historical Commission. This plaque was placed by the Trail Marker Tree on Canterbury Court.

This is a photo of the Chalk on Masonite by Warner Sallman (famous artist known for his portrait of Christ), done in 1939. Dennis and his assistant, with the help of a Sallman collector, were able to track down this artistic piece and locate it at the North Park University. Courtesy of Covenant Archives and Historical Library, North Park University, Chicago, Illinois.

Mr. Downes and Susan Macon at Mr. Downes' Trail Marker Tree Exhibit in the Northbrook Historical Museum.

Mr. J.L. Kraft's daughter Edith and her husband standing on the Trail marker Tree on Canterbury Court in front of their home. Photo courtesy of Susan Macon.

This photo of the plat of the original Wilmette Village was included in Herbert Mulford's book, *Wilmette and the Suburban Whirl: A Sequel to "Frontiers of Old Wilmette,"* Mulford was responsible for much of the

research behind Wilmette's project honoring the Greenwood Avenue and Canterbury Court Trail Marker Trees.

Jake McDaniel, mail carrier and grandson of the first postmaster in that suburb, is shown pointing the way next to the Greenwood Avenue Trail Marker Tree. This photo was taken by a staff photographer of a local paper.

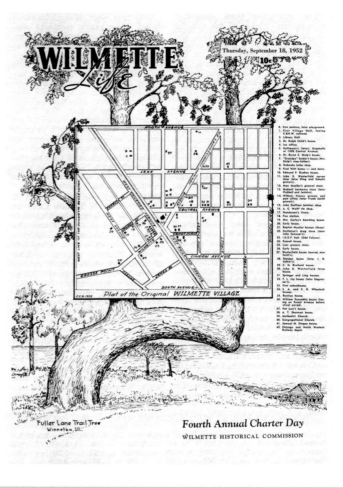

Susan's mother, Edith, was the only daughter of J.L. Kraft of Kraft Foods.

A Trail Marker Tree that is located near Gillson Park is still standing today. This double trunk Trail Marker Tree is located on private property and only has one upright limb remaining. The tree stands nearly next to the home on the property and the original builders actually made special accommodations while building the home to save the tree.

The Winnetka Trail Marker Tree Shaping Project

In 2007, Robert Smith, the superintendent of parks, contacted Mr. Downes regarding a project to shape Trail Marker Trees in significant areas of the village. Three separate locations were chosen to plant and shape the trees. The author collaborated with Robert Smith and assistant Amanda Braus of the Winnetka Park District, longtime resident Joe Fell, and Patti Van Cleave of the Winnetka Historical Society throughout this project. *The Winnetka Historical Society Gazette* recently wrote an article about this project in which the Historical Society was quoted, "We are so pleased to be a part of this project, as it will allow future generations to be aware of those that inhabited the area long ago." More recently, in June 2010, the Historical Society requested Mr. Downes' knowledge and expertise of the Trail Marker Trees be applied for the shaping of a Trail Marker Tree at the Historical Society itself.

This non-typical, hickory, Trail Marker Tree is still standing in Winnetka on private property. The owners of the property attended one of Mr. Downes' Trail Marker Tree exhibits and invited him to photograph the tree. This tree is over 200 years old and has been referenced as a Trail Marker Tree by Raymond Janssen and other experts. Photo taken by Downes Research Team.

Mr. Downes in front of the Winnetka Historical Society.

This permanent plaque has been placed near one of the young trees Dennis shaped in collaboration with the Winnetka Park District and the Winnetka Historical Society.

Mr. Downes and Robert Smith, superintendent of parks, standing in front of one of the newly shaped Trail Marker Trees in Winnetka. Photo courtesy of the *Winnetka Historical Society Gazette*.

The Cumnor Road Tree

One of the most well-known Trail Marker Trees that stood in Kenilworth was the Cumnor Road tree, which stood until recent years when it fell in a vicious storm. In an article written by Ted Gregory and Susan Kuczkak, John Callahan (the current owner of the property where the Cumnor Road tree stood) said, "It's been written up in all the history books about Kenilworth. And the Girl Scouts and all the kids in elementary school would make pilgrimages to see it." While this might sound like a proud property owner, the tree was in fact mentioned in many publications for example, *Joseph Sears and His Kenilworth*, 1969; *First Fifty Years, Village of Kenilworth*, 1947; and *Wilmette Life*, 1948; along with many others. The author first saw this tree in the 1960's and was later reintroduced to it in 2002 by Northbrook resident, Glen Roberts. Roberts was a parent and chaperone at Mr. Downes' exhibit at the Grove Redfield Estate in 2002, at which Mr. Downes' treated Glenbrook North High School Students to an early private showing and lecture on the Trail Marker Trees. The attending teacher, Lee Block, said, "...*let me take the opportunity to thank you once again for your time and effort spent with my students prior to your opening night. I think it truly was a rich experience for me as well as my students meeting you and seeing your work...*" Thanks to Mr. Roberts, Dennis was able to revisit this tree and take current photos before it fell.

Kenilworth had three other known Trail Marker Trees in addition to the Cumnor Road tree. Two Marker Trees stood at the corner of Oxford and Warwick, and another Trail Marker Tree stood on Kenilworth Avenue. In an old newspaper article written in *Wilmette Life*, it is said the tree that stood at 237 Kenilworth Avenue was the second oldest known tree in the town. The article also says, *"How blessed that this old Trail Tree should be beside the boyhood home of Bentley McCloud adjoining the home of his grandchildren, a fourth generation family growing up in Kenilworth, for we know it will be cherished."* Bentley McCloud was the Kenilworth Historical Society's President in 1931.

Evanston

A little further south, down the beautiful shoreline, lays the town of Evanston. *"At practically every corner in Evanston, there is some kind of a roadmarker to guide the more than 100,000 people who drive in and through the city every day. Evanston's first road markers were trees that the Indians bent and tied down, thus permanently deforming them."* (Centennial Book, 1951)

Due to Evanston's early rapid growth, many of these Trail Marker Trees that were prevalent throughout the area quickly disappeared. In the book, *Evanston, Its Land and Its People*, 1928, published by the Fort Dearborn Chapter Daughters of the American Revolution, the author V.C. Reeling mentions that only oak trees were used as Trail Marker Trees in the Evanston area. One oak Indian Marker Tree stood on Davis Street and Hinman Avenue, another red oak stood near the Cavalry Cemetery. Thankfully, through the efforts of the Daughters of

This is an old photograph taken by J.L. Graff of Chicago, of the Triple Trunk Trail Marker Tree when it was still living at the Cavalry Station/Cemetery.

At The Grove's Redfield Center, Dennis Downes talks about his work with Glenbrook North students William McIntosh, left, and Trevor Roberts, right. This photo was taken by Geoff Scheerer in 2002 of the Pioneer Press to be used in the article, "Art Students meet Famed Alum."

This photograph of historian, Frank R. Grover, appeared in History of Evanston, Illinois, 1906.

This photo is an old photograph of the Cumnor Road Trail Marker Tree that was shown in the book, Joseph Sears and His Kenilworth, 1969.

This photo was taken by the author of the Cumnor Road Trail Marker Tree in 2002.

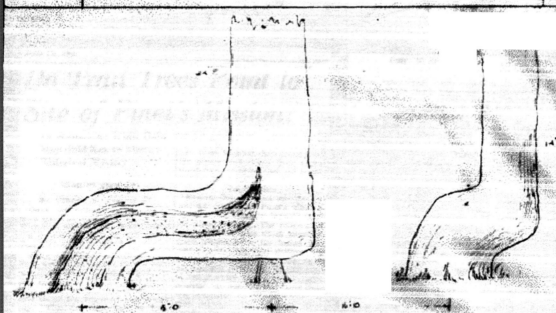

90' West of ⊄ Cumnor Rd 200' N. of ⊄ Kenilworth Ave. Points N.W.

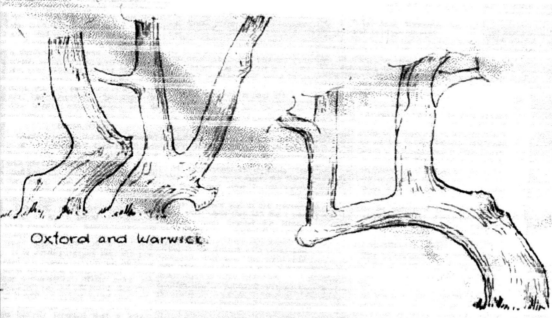

Oxford and Warwick

191 Fuller Lane, Winnetka.
Points E., N.E.

This is a copy of sketches (provided by the Evanston Historical Society) that refer to some of the known Kenilworth Trail Marker Trees from the past. It also includes a sketch of the Fuller Lane tree.

This photograph was taken of the Triple Trunk Trail Marker Tree after it was moved to the park on Davis Street and placed as a monument. This photograph appeared in an article by Raymond Janssen, Indian Trail Trees, 1934.

the American Revolution, one of these historical landmarks, the red oak, was saved and turned into a monument, so that it too would not be lost. This Triple Trunk Trail Marker Tree, according to Raymond Janssen, originally stood on the Green Bay Trail, just west of the Cavalry Station and pointed to the largest Indian village in the area, known then as Bowmanville. It was later moved to a park at Sheridan Road and Davis Street in 1926 by the D.A.R. where it stood as a monument. In the 1980s, the author attended a meeting at the Great Lakes Region Historical Society, where he was able to speak to a member of the local Potawatomi tribe that confirmed his belief that the Triple Trunk Trail Marker Trees were in fact used to indicate areas of habitation or villages. One of the first in the Evanston area to spark an interest in the Trail Marker Trees was Frank R. Grover, the vice president of the Evanston Historical Society. Grover's father was one of the pioneers of Cook County who came to Chicago in 1844. He addressed the Chicago Historical Society in 1905 with his paper on Indian Trail Marker Trees. Another member of the Evanston Historical Society and vice president of the Chicago Academy of Sciences, Charles S. Raddin, was said to have taken a great interest in these trees. A.W. Watriss of Rogers Park was one of the first to take photographs of Trail Marker Trees in this area, according to the *History of Evanston, Illinois*, 1906. The interest created by these early historians helped lead to the D.A.R.'s formation of a committee and funding for the placement of one of the first bronze tablets marking this Evanston Trail Marker Tree and monument.

On this tablet was inscribed, *"This red oak was a Potawatomi trail tree which grew on Green Bay Trail immediately west of Cavalry Station where it pointed to a large Indian Village located on and east of the site of Bowmanville."* This monument stood proudly in the park for decades until 1955, seen and visited by thousands. The D.A.R.'s efforts not only here, but across the country, have helped to preserve Native American landmarks and history. The author was fortunate to verify these efforts by the D.A.R. with the help of the Regent of the Fort Dearborn Chapter, Edith Trutter Hauff.

The Ridgemoor Country Club

The Ridgemoor Country Club, one of the oldest country clubs in northern Chicago, is home to one of the oldest Indian Trail Marker Trees still living in the area. In 1910, artist George E. Colby created an illustration of this directional Trail Marker Tree that pointed eastward towards Lake Michigan. This Trail Marker Tree was upon what would become the Indian Boundary Line created by the Prairie du Chien treaty between the United States and the Chippewa, Ottawa, and Potawatomi Indians. Downes was informed about the possibility of this tree still being alive in early 2000 by a young man visiting one of his Trail Marker Tree exhibits held at the Grove Redfield Estate. This young man had a great interest in the Trail Marker Trees of the area, and he gave the author the name of the Country Club where this tree was supposed to be located. The following winter Dennis planned a visit with his wife, Gail, to the Ridgemoor Country Club, choosing to go in the winter to have better visibility of the trees. After having no luck locating the tree, a chance meeting with Mr. E. J. Hobson occurred, (at the time, he was the oldest member of the country club,) and the author was able to locate the tree with Mr. Hobson's help. Mr. Hobson informed Dennis that the Trail Marker Tree was difficult to see because the ground had been built up around the tree to create a berm. This bur oak Trail Marker Tree still stands today.

Morton Grove

While Morton Grove was home to many Trail Marker Trees, one in the Miami Woods that is still standing today and another Marker Tree have received lots of attention from the Morton Grove Historical Museum, Morton Grove Historical Society, and Morton Grove Park District. Unfortunately, this Marker Tree has also been partially buried during the construction of the nearby Nashville Avenue. The author met Mary Busch, from the Morton Grove Historical Museum, at one of his early Trail Marker Tree exhibits, where she informed him of a Marker Tree that their society had worked to protect. Jayne Barry's family, Morton Grove resident, had a long history with this Marker Tree. Her family settled on the land where the tree stood in 1868, and her grandmother protected the tree and passed on her knowledge of the tree to her granddaughter, Jayne. The village of Morton Grove had planned to cut down the tree to turn Nashville Avenue into a two-way street, Jayne and the Historical Society acted quickly to save the tree.

This is a photograph of the Clubhouse taken in 1905; the Trail Marker Tree can be seen visibly above the ground standing in front of the clubhouse. Photo courtesy of the Ridgemoor Country Club.

This is a photograph of the illustration by George E. Colby depicting the Ridgemoor Trail Marker Tree, completed in 1910.

Mr. Downes shown next to the Ridgemoor Trail Marker Tree since it has been partially covered by the berm. Photo by Gail Spreen.

Photograph of Mr. Downes standing in front of the now partially buried, Morton Grove Marker Tree. Photo by Mary Busch, historian.

This photo is of Jayne Barry, age 85 at the time of the photo in the 1990s. Jayne is 'standing guard' next to the Morton Grove Marker Tree that her grandmother also protected over 100 years before. Photo by Waldemar Reichert, article by S.U. Mahesh.

A meeting was held between Mary Walsh and Mary Busch of the Historical Museum, Jim DeHorn of the Openlands Project Treekeeper, and John Thill, the president of the Friends of the Morton Grove Forest Preserve to verify the age of the Marker Tree that was being protected by the Historical Society. After much calculation, it was determined that the tree was approximately 214 years old (in 2004) and thus was old enough to be considered an authentic Indian Marker Tree. This particular type of Marker Tree is referred to by Raymond Janssen in an article, *Living Guide Posts of the Past*, 1941. This tree still stands today and remains protected by the citizens of Morton Grove.

Northbrook

Originally, the town of Northbrook was named Shermerville, named after Fredrick Schermer, who donated the land for the town's first railroad station. In 1921, the town held a renaming contest. A man named Edward Landwehr submitted the name "Northbrook," which became the winner and the town was officially named Northbrook by 1923. Although Shermerville does not have as many recorded trees as the surrounding towns, it can be assumed they were there and simply not documented like the trees in the surrounding towns. There are, however, a few references to Shermerville in regards to Marker Trees and Trail Marker Trees. In 1912, John Halsey, LL.D. mentions a great Marker Tree that served as a guide post for the area. Later Jens Jensen makes reference to a Trail Maker Tree off the North Branch of the Chicago River in the area.

There are documented Trail Marker Trees in Glencoe, east of the town; Deerfield, north of the town; and Glenview, south of the town. From the author's extensive research, it has become apparent that the majority of Trail Marker Trees were never recorded. Downes believes we should be grateful for the few that have been recorded and documented. In fact, in the early 1900s Raymond Gloede had the most extensive photographic collection of Trail Marker Trees that he shared with researchers, including over 300 photographs of trees from Illinois and the surrounding states. Unfortunately, nearly all of his photographs were destroyed.

While born in Chicago, Dennis moved with his family to unincorporated Northbrook in 1951 and remained there until the late 1960s. While living in Northbrook, the author saw a Trail Marker Tree for the first time along the shores of Lake Michigan. Later, Dennis would discuss these trees with his Uncle John Downes, who lived nearby on Walters Avenue. John Downes further explained the significance of these trees and how they were used to aid in land and water navigation. John S. Clark, a Northbrook resident, whose family resided in the area since the mid 1800's, also added to the author's early knowledge of other Trail Marker Trees in surrounding areas. Local Boy Scout Troops were taken on trips to see the known Trail Marker Trees and often told Dennis about their experiences. It would be more than 30 years later in 2003, after moving away from Northbrook, that the author would receive a phone call from the chairman of the Northbrook

The author and artist standing with Scot and Lori Pepper in front of the 16' Trail Marker Tree Sculpture at the Buchholz Property where it would be filmed by the Northbrook Arts Commission for NCTV. The Peppers are longtime supporters of the Trail Marker Tree project.

Dennis handling the ropes as the Trail Marker Tree sculpture was properly positioned to be moved to Wildlife Prairie State Park.

Downes and Michael Gorman, actor and director, who filmed the documentary on the author and his work with the Trail Marker Trees.

The author and artist in the final stages of creating his 16' Realistic Trail Marker Tree Sculpture.

Friends of the author helping to position the tree at the Buchholz Property, from the left: John Heineman, Greg Prochnow, Keith Schultz, Todd, Perry Crakes, Don Schreiber, and Brian Buchholz.

Arts Commission. They had chosen his work to be filmed for a 30-minute documentary to air on cable television. This documentary featured the first life-sized, realistic Trail Marker Tree sculpture and his study of the trees. The video was filmed by Michael Gorman of NCTV, Channel 17. Gorman, actor and film director also conducted the interview with the author. After watching the documentary, Judy Hughes the president of the Northbrook Historical Society and chairman of the Northbrook Arts Commission said, *"The 30-minute video you did for the Northbrook Arts Commission is as interesting to watch for the 10th time as it was the first time. In fact, each time I see it I learn something else about your research, t he magnificent trail trees..."* The documentary was completed just before the sculpture was moved to the Wildlife Prairie State Park in Peoria, Illinois. The 16-foot Trail Marker Tree sculpture had been accepted as a finalist in the National/ International juried exhibition to be held at the park from June 15th, 2003 through October 15, 2003; other famous artists included Cheri Cappello and Bruce White. This exhibition was called "Art on the Prairie" and was organized by Dr. Harry and Karly Spell, owners of Adagio Fine Art and Art Casting of Illinois. In a full page article in the *Journal Star*, titled "A Tree Marks the Spot" by Clare Howard, Dr. Harry Spell was quoted saying, *"For both painting and sculpture, Downes conducts exhaustive research"* remarking on *"his dedication to education as well as to pure form in art."* Downes' educational and historical sculpture made an impression on

Lisa Holmes, the general manager of the park, said, *"Children are especially fascinated by the Trail Marker Tree. Families come to the park to learn about animals and nature, and now they are learning more than that."* According to Lisa, thousands of visitors viewed the sculpture and the educational plaque that the author put up to accompany the sculpture. Downes also supplied the park with educational Trail Marker Tree brochures that were handed out during the five-month exhibition.

Several years later in 2008, the Northbrook Historical Museum would host the author's largest Trail Marker Tree exhibit to date, featuring his five-foot bronze Trail Marker Tree sculpture. This exhibit also featured a photographic collection of Trail Marker Trees, both past and present, from the author's study spanning three decades and over 40 states. *"Museum visitors who are now fans, have enjoyed this step back in time to learn through photographs and sculpture about the first directional signage in America,"* said the president of the Northbrook Historical Society. During this four-month exhibit, Judy Hughes shared a childhood story with Dennis, remembering how she too had visited Trail Marker Trees in the North Shore area with her Girl Scout Troop. After the Trail Marker Tree exhibit, Downes' five-foot bronze sculpture was accepted into the Lakefront Sculpture Exhibition and put on display for an entire year in downtown Chicago. During this exhibition, the author also installed an educational plaque to accompany his Trail Marker Tree sculpture and conducted lectures at the site where the sculpture was installed.

Researcher and artist Dennis Downes of Lake County stands in front of his sculpture "Trail Marker Tree" recently at Wildlife Prairie State Park. Photo by Leslie Renken and text by Clare Howard of the Journal Star, Peoria.

This photograph was sent to the author by the Emanuel family after they had visited his sculpture and read the educational plaque at the Wildlife Prairie State Park. They located this Trail Marker Tree on their property near Dunlap, Illinois. Included beneath the photo is the actual string they used to measure the circumference of the tree and mailed to Downes to verify the measurements.

Part of the photographic exhibit at the Northbrook Historical Museum, 2008.

Downes giving an explanation of the well-known Exmoor Trail Marker Tree during his exhibit at the Northbrook Historical Museum.

The Northbrook Historical Museum building, once the Northfield Inn, built in circa 1894 and stood at the corner of Shermer Road and Waukegan Road, also known to some as Bartelme's. It was moved to its present day location near the Village Green Park in 1975.

The author still has a strong connection to his childhood home and friends, both from his grade school, St. Norbert's, and Glenbrook North High School.

Glenview

Glenview is another beautiful and historical town, only miles from the shores of Lake Michigan. One of Glenview's first residents was John Kennicott; his son Robert Kennicott would later be recognized for his contributions in the scientific community. The Kennicott's moved to The Grove in 1836, at the time an 886-acre property near the Des Plaines River, also referred to as The Grove Portage. The Indian name for the Des Plaines River is 'she shick ma wash sippe,' meaning soft maple tree river. The Grove is now a National Historic Landmark; it contains an interpretive center, moved and re-created historic buildings (including the original home of John Kennicott), and nature trails. Due to the efforts of the Frog and Fern Ladies and their formation of the Save the Grove Committee, The Grove was officially dedicated as a Historic Landmark by the U.S. Department of the Interior in 1976. A biographer introduced Robert Kennicott and The Grove as thus: "Here he grew up, a frail, child, with little formal schooling, but with the good fortune of association with his father, who was notable both as a physician and as a horticulturalist, and so also with a wide acquaintance of his parents' friends, who included most of the intellectual leaders of the community. This very freedom from formal schooling, with its encouragement

of time spent in the woods and on the prairies and marshes, shaped his interest in natural history." (Courtesy of Steve Swanson, The Grove Redfield Estate) At the young age of 17, Robert conducted a series of experiments on the effects of rattlesnake venom with Dr. Daniel Brainard; Robert was responsible for collecting the venomous snakes. Dr. Brainard of Chicago was the founder of Rush Medical College and named the college in honor of Dr. Benjamin Rush. Dr. Rush was the only doctor that had attended medical school to also sign the Declaration of Independence. He also taught the basic medical skills to Meriwether Lewis, before his expedition with William Clark (Lewis and Clark Expedition, 1804-1806). Robert Kennicott was known for helping to found the Chicago Academy of Sciences, where he later served as secretary, curator, trustee, and finally director. Kennicott also helped to establish the museum at Northwestern University; it opened with a collection that he had obtained during a three-month field study, he later served as curator for the museum. Kennicott achieved many other great things in his lifetime and his influences on the scientific community and world of natural history will never be forgotten.

The Trail Marker Trees in the Glenview area were no secret; they were well documented and studied by many experts. The most famous Marker Tree in the area was the Potawatomi Tree (the Black Hawk Tree) that was located on the border of Glenview. One of the foremost authorities on the Kennicott Family, Steve Swanson, director of The Grove stated, *"Robert*

Downes lecturing at the site of his Bronze Trail Marker Tree Sculpture during the Lakefront Sculpture Exhibition Tour Event in October, 2009. The tree was located on Sheridan Road in front of the Gill Park .

Artist and researcher Downes signing autographs for fans at the Lakefront Sculpture Exhibition Opening Night Event, sponsored by Alderman Vi Daley and Alderman Tom Tunney.

A photograph of the educational plaque that Downes made with his assistant to accompany the Bronze Trail Marker Tree Sculpture for the yearlong display.

Early photo of Robert Kennicott, the explorer and naturalist. Photo courtesy of Steve Swanson, Director of The Grove.

Portrait of Robert Kennicott, who helped found the Chicago Academy of Sciences and promoted its growth and success. Kennicott also helped establish the museum at Northwestern University. Photo courtesy of Steve Swanson, director of The Grove.

TRAIL MARKER TREE SCULPTURE
BY: DENNIS DOWNES

The sculpture presented here, on the limestone boulder, was inspired by nearly three decades of research and study of Trail Marker Trees by the Artist. Trail Trees were an ancient form of land navigation that were used by many of the Native American tribes and later by fur traders, missionaries, and early pioneers. These trees were shaped as saplings by bending the trunks into a distinctive shape to point direction. The Trail Marker Trees would point the way to specific places such as fresh water springs, mineral deposits, areas of exposed stone and copper, and areas where medicinal plants would grow. You can think of the Trail Trees much like we think of exit signs off of our major highways today. While the Native Americans knew the major paths and routes they used for trading and hunting; the Trail Marker Trees acted as their exit signs, guiding them to points of more specific needs. The Trail Trees have been found and documented all across the United States; however, the Chicago Land and surrounding areas were fortunate to have some of the earliest documented Trail Trees. The Chicago born Artist was introduced to the Trail Marker Trees as a young boy. he was able to see living Trail Trees along the north shore of Lake Michigan that have long since disappeared. Since then he has spent nearly thirty years of his adult life researching the Trail Trees in over thirty states, hosting exhibits and giving over one hundred lectures to the public on the history of the Trail Trees. The goal of the Artist is to have his Trail Marker Tree sculptures placed in areas of historical significance to commemorate this ingenious form of land navigation used by the Native Americans so that these historical icons are never forgotten.

Mr. Downes would like to thank the Lakefront Sculpture Exhibition, Alderman Vi Daley, Alderman Tom Tunney, and The East Lakeview Neighbors for giving him the opportunity to exhibit this sculpture in Chicago.

downesstudio.net
Downes Studio. All Rights Reserved.

Kennicott grew up at The Grove and walked in the forests with the Potawatomi Indians. He traveled the Indian trails and used the trail trees to navigate. As his explorations increased in ever-growing concentric circles he made irreplaceable collections and vocabularies of the native North American people." Swanson also provided the quote, *"I have, of course, received a new name by which I am called by the Indians. It is Che-tsoh-kah-kieh..."* Robert Kennicott, July 3, 1861, the name was defined as 'bird chief.' Frank Grover, in 1905, wrote about Trail Marker Trees located near what is now called the Glenview Golf Club. One of these trees was actually a bur oak Marker Tree that was marking the location of an Indian Village. Another of these trees, located on the North Branch of the Chicago River, was marking the portage route from the North Branch of the Chicago River towards the Des Plaines River. Later in 1940, Raymond Janssen would also refer to the Trail Maker Trees of Glenview and specifically the triple trunk Marker Tree that marked an Indian Village that Grover previously discussed.

During Downes' research, a childhood friend of his brother, Daniel Martin, would introduce Downes to Carol Ann Busche who had a Trail Marker Tree on her property. Mrs. Busche now lives on what is referred to as Portage Run, a private lane; this was part of the original 886 acres that the Kennicott family owned many years ago. The home the Busche Family lives in was designed by Frank Lloyd Wright in 1950, originally for the Carr Family. Mr. Edward Busche, Carol Ann's

husband, was also a respected architect. The home was designed to be environmentally conscious, with the eave of the home built around a massive oak that still stands today. The Busche Family was told about the Directional Trail Marker Tree on their property by Donald C. Peattie. The massive bur oak was said to be one of the trees that guided the portage trail to the Des Plaines River. This tree too, like so many others, has died and no longer can be seen. Carol Ann Busche personally told the author about the tree and showed Downes where it used to stand on the property.

Donald C. Peattie married into the Redfield Family to John Kennicott's great granddaughter, Louise, and had lived in the Redfield Estate himself in the 1930's. Donald C. Peattie worked for the U.S. Department of Agriculture; he was a botanist, naturalist, and author. Peattie attended the University of Chicago and transferred to Harvard, where he graduated in 1922. In one of Peattie's books, *A Natural History of Trees of Eastern and Central North America* (1948), in his section about bur oaks he writes "...*old portage trees of this species, bent down by the Indians a century and more ago, in their sapling stage, to mark the canoe carries from one of the slow historic rivers or lakes to the next...*" Peattie's writings were known to be distinguished and scientifically scrupulous.

Another Trail Marker Tree, located just off of the Des Plaines River, was the last tree in the portage trail, connecting the Chicago River North Branch to the Des Plaines River. Steve Swanson's personal account of this tree follows,

"*I still remember as a kid the large Indian Trail Tree located near Beck Lake in the Cook County Forest Preserve. It appeared to be the first marker when you entered the Grove Portage Trail from the Des Plains River that led thru Kennicott's Grove and then continued east to the North Branch of the Chicago River...*" According to Swanson, the bur oak tree had fallen by 1986. The Trail Maker Trees on this portage trail clearly marked the Native Americans' route between the Des Plaines River and the North Branch of the Chicago River. Up until this point, these trees had not been recognized forming the Grove Portage Trail; they had only been documented individually. The author was able to connect this line of trees creating The Grove Portage Trail through extensive research, field study, and knowledge from his time spent living at The Grove. During the author's research, he was able to locate the Scharf Manuscript from the early 1900s. In this manuscript, Albert F. Scharf refers directly to "The Grove portage of the Indians" where at the western end were the signal fire pit and the portage camp. References like this helped Dennis piece together the importance of the Portage Trail Marker Trees.

Shortly before The Grove was dedicated as a National Landmark, Dennis actually lived there in the early 1970s. During this time he was able to learn a great deal of history about The Grove and Robert Kennicott. It would be 30 years later that Dennis' friend, Jude Kitts, of Glenview, would introduce him to Steve Swanson and he would return to The Grove to show his Trail Marker Tree exhibit to the

This photograph, taken by the author, shows the cecreopia silkmoth (giant moth). This moth was sacred to the Illiniwek tribe and used as a sacred symbol.

This is a photo of the Triple Trunk Trail Marker Tree that pointed to a nearby Indian Village. The photo was shown in an article by Raymond Janssen.

Downes with Steve Swanson, director of The Grove, and Carol Di Lorenzo, coordinator of The Grove showing one of Downes' small bronze Trail Marker Tree sculptures.

A photograph of Downes' bronze Trail Marker Tree Sculpture standing in The Grove great room, taken from outside. This bronze was part of Downes' educational exhibit.

public of Glenview. Since that time, his exhibit has been held there every year for the past decade. Through large public exhibits like this, the author was able to have personal contact with hundreds of visitors each year. Some of these visitors brought information that led to the author discovering other Trail Marker Trees, articles, and photographs. After one of Downes' exhibits Carol Di Lorenzo, The Grove coordinator, stated, *"We admire your knowledge and talent and appreciate the opportunity to share our location to host this event. The extensive trail marker tree exhibit shows your dedication to the research you have spent so many years detailing and collecting. Many visitors have learned of this historic legacy for the first time. It is truly a pleasure to be part of it and especially to see so many people from all walks of life enjoy your work."* In 2005, Downes celebrated the anniversary of his 100th public exhibit at The Grove; people from across the country attended this event. Gary Donatelli, Emmy Award-Winning-Director, camera man, and teacher flew from New York to visit this exhibit. After viewing the exhibit, Donatelli remarked, *"The Grove in Glenview was a perfect setting for the 100th show of Mr. Downes' work. Set back in the trees on a rustic manor, his work, which is a reflection of the nature around us, was right at home. The work reflects a knowledge and reverence for the Native Americans who were here long before the Europeans...Also fascinating was the display of Trail Marker Trees and their significance...The large crowd was a testament to the popularity of this important artist/anthropologist."*

The following poem was a reaction to the Trail Marker Tree exhibit at The Grove, experienced for the first time by a guest, brought by longtime supporters Patti and Jeff Steinback for the author's 10th Anniversary Exhibit.

The Trail Marker Tree

The hands were laid, the stakes secured,
to hold the sapling firm,
then father Time applied his will,
in process for a term.

To bind in cause, and stay in form,
but change in height and girth—
this wonderwork of nature,
set to point the way on earth.

A pathway guide – a journey's aid,
a symbol poised to show,
the way to destinations—
in the dark and in the snow.

By language known to some—
and yet to others a mystery,
the friend of Natives and to Downes,
The Trail Marker Tree.

Donald W. Hecox, JC

Photos depicting part of the author's photographic Trail Marker Tree exhibit at The Grove.

The Grove 100th Anniversary show, showing (from the left) Perry Hansen, Dennis Downes, Michael Gorman, Jim English, and Gary Donatelli.

Photograph of The Grove Redfield House taken during one of Downes' exhibits. This is the house that Donald C. Peattie would have resided in during the 1930's.

This photo shows the author's assistant, Liz Fox, standing next to the bronze Trail Marker Tree Sculpture, shown first at The Grove and later at the Chicago Lakefront.

Photograph of Albert Joseph of Northbrook, IL.

Another longtime supporter, Albert Joseph of Northbrook, brilliant writer and president of Hunter Publishing, also visited The Grove exhibit on a regular basis, as did his son George and daughter Janelle. Mr. Joseph was a world traveler, avid outdoorsman, history buff, and scholar. Mr. Joseph's passion for the Lewis and Clark Expedition (Corps of Discovery) and personal experiences in the outdoors helped him to understand the need for the Trail Marker Trees. At several of The Grove exhibits, Mr. Joseph and the author had in-depth conversations about the use of Trail Marker Trees, upright stones, and petroglyphs by Indian guides and scouts throughout the United States. Mr. Joseph was so influenced by history and the outdoors that his last request was for his ashes to be spread at Pompey's Pillar, a landmark of the Lewis and Clark Expedition. When Mr. Joseph recently passed, a quote from Merriwether Lewis was included on his commemorative card written by his children.

The Glenview area, especially The Grove, has had a great impact on the author's study of the Trail Marker Trees. The history of Robert Kennicott helped to inspire him to pursue this study through the course of his life and the support of The Grove and its staff today helping to further the cause.

Glencoe

Glencoe, once known as Taylorsport named for its first non-native family, is located along the shore of Lake Michigan and is known for its majestic bluffs and scenic shoreline.

This town is home to the Chicago Botanic Garden, a remarkable place of ever changing natural beauty. Near Glencoe's scenic shores was where the author saw some of his first Trail Marker Trees as a boy. The Glencoe area has several documented Trail Marker Trees and a Council Tree; there is also a special form of the Trail Marker Trees that are common to this area. This special form of Trail Marker Tree was photographed by Bess Dunn, discussed by Frank Grover and John Halsey LL.D., and written about and explained by Raymond Janssen in 1940, *"Occasionally when no young tree happened to be growing in a spot where a trail marker was desired, the Indians resorted to the bending of the lowermost branch of an older tree. The effect upon that particular branch was similar; the branch put forth new side branches which extended upward at an odd angle from the main one."* Another reason this type of Trail Marker Tree was used, as pointed out by Janssen in the article, Living Guide Posts of the Past, was that the Indians could make these markers as conspicuous or as inconspicuous as desired.

Four of these Trail Marker Trees were located off of the Green Bay Trail, near the Union/Pacific North Railway route. A Trail Marker Tree of this form was located on the southern border of Glencoe, an area that used to be called Lakeside. This tree was photographed by the Chicago Historical Society and the photo was used in the *Book of the North Shore*, 1910. The next example in this line would appear a little farther north off the Green Bay Trail, just east of the Lakefront Park.

This huge bur oak is still standing today. One of these trees, after which the nearby Indian Tree Drive was named, could actually be seen from the train passing by and became well known by the locals and commuters. Another similarly shaped Trail Marker Tree was located just to the north along the trail, near what today is the intersection of Dean Avenue and St. John's Avenue. These four Trail Marker Trees were all shaped nearly identically and located along the Green Bay Trail through the town of Glencoe. A fifth example of this type of Trail Marker Tree was included in the article *Living Guide Posts of the Past*. Unfortunately, the exact location was not included and the tree is no longer living. The earliest reference to these trees was on a federal survey in 1838; this survey was mentioned in *A History of Lake County* by John Halsey LL.D. in 1912.

One Trail Marker Tree located at the northern most point of Cook County, in Glencoe, was one of the first Trail Marker Trees to ever be commemorated with a bronze tablet. This tablet was placed by the D.A.R. in 1911 and was inscribed:

This Indian Trail Tree, at the northern boundary of Cook County, is the most noticeable one standing on a highway. There are eleven similarly bent trees in Cook County pointing the direction of the Indian trails. The branch was bent and fastened to the ground by the Indians when the tree was a sapling...
This tree is near the Green Bay Trail, later the wagon road of the early white settlers of the 1830 period, followed, as a further advance in civilization, by the Chicago and Northwestern R.R.

Photograph of Dennis at the shores of Glencoe Beach overlooking magnificent Lake Michigan.

Photograph by the author showing an example of the type of Trail Marker Tree Raymond Janssen was referring to in his 1940 article. This photo depicts the drastically bent limb.

This photograph, courtesy of the Chicago Historical Society, is from the book, *Book of the North Shore* by Marian White in 1910. It shows a Trail Marker Tree standing in the area that used to be referred to as Lakeside in the late 1800s.

This photograph shows one of the Trail Marker Trees along the railroad tracks, following the old Green Bay Trail.

This Trail Marker Tree is standing just east of Lakefront Park in Glencoe.

1853, and later by the Chicago and Milwaukee electric R.R. 1899. This tablet is erected by the Chicago Chapter, Daughters of the American Revolution, May 6 1911, to encourage interest in local history, and perpetuate the memory of the disappearing Indian race.

A more traditional Trail Marker Tree, according to Raymond Gloede, was located just north of Dundee Road near Vernon Avenue. This huge tree was also just off of the Green Bay Trail. The Glencoe Chapter of the Daughters of the American Revolution led by Mrs. Anna Ickes organized a special ceremony to honor this Trail Marker Tree. Mrs. Ickes' husband, Harold, was the Secretary of the Department of the Interior and was involved with the Skokie Lagoon Project. The ceremony included the placing of a bronze tablet in 1928 and was attended by several representatives of the Native Americans, local historians (including Gloede), and local boy scouts. The plaque was inscribed:

"This Indian Trail Tree Marked a New Pathway Thru the Forest, the Hunting Ground of the Indian Tribes, Along the Shores of Lake Michigan. Tablet Placed by the Glencoe Chapter, Daughters of the American Revolution 1928"

This ceremony, through the efforts of the Glencoe Chapter D.A.R., drew a great deal of attention to this and other surrounding Trail Marker Trees for decades to come.

THIS INDIAN TRAIL TREE,

AT THE NORTHERN BOUNDARY OF COOK COUNTY, IS THE MOST NOTICEABLE ONE STANDING ON A HIGHWAY. THERE ARE ELEVEN SIMILARLY BENT TREES IN COOK COUNTY, POINTING THE DIRECTION OF THE INDIAN TRAILS. THE BRANCH WAS BENT AND FASTENED TO THE GROUND BY THE INDIANS, WHEN THE TREE WAS A SAPLING, OVER 80 YEARS AGO. THIS TREE IS NEAR THE GREEN BAY TRAIL, LATER THE WAGON ROAD OF THE EARLY WHITE SETTLERS OF THE 1830 PERIOD, FOLLOWED, AS A FURTHER ADVANCE IN CIVILIZATION, BY THE CHICAGO & NORTHWESTERN R.R. 1855, AND LATER BY THE CHICAGO & MILWAUKEE ELECTRIC R.R. 1899. THIS TABLET IS ERECTED BY THE CHICAGO CHAPTER, DAUGHTERS OF THE AMERICAN REVOLUTION, MAY 6, 1911, TO ENCOURAGE INTEREST IN LOCAL HISTORY, AND PERPETUATE THE MEMORY OF THE DISAPPEARING INDIAN RACE.

This photo depicts a special ceremony honoring a Glencoe Trail Marker Tree. The Daughters of the American Revolution, specifically Mrs. Anna Ickes, helped to make this event possible. An Indian Chief as well as two other Native Americans from the Wisconsin Dells area attended as well as university students, boy scouts, and local historians. This photograph was taken by Mr. Goede in 1928. This photo was located with the help of the Winnetka Historical Society.

This photo shows the bronze plaque that was placed at the northern most Trail Marker Tree in Glencoe. This photo is courtesy of the Highland Park Historical Society, archivist Nancy Webster, and the Highland Park News.

This is a photo of the entrance to the Chicago Botanic Garden, a place renowned for its beauty.

Photograph of the Millard "Log House" in May of 2001 before the restoration process began-Robert Swanson (pictured in front of the home) invited the author to view the home and walk the property before the renovations began. Photo taken by author.

The Glencoe area also has two Marker Trees. One unusual Marker Tree that stands in the Botanic Garden needs further study. It strongly resembles the famous "Old Oak" that stood near University Hall at Northwestern University. This tree was first brought to the author's attention by volunteers working at the Botanic Garden and a local history teacher who actually brought photos for Dennis to view at one of the Trail Marker Tree exhibits. Close to the Lake Michigan shore is another highly unusual and old oak tree that is said to be a Marker Tree. While researching this tree, still standing on private property, the property owner informed the author about a children's book entitled *A Tree's Tale* by Lark Carrier. Over 10 years later, Dennis would finally track down this book through the interlibrary loan system. This book, although a children's book, discussed some serious issues. Specifically, how the Trail Marker Tree in this book was saved from loggers and ship builders.

In the early years of this country, when America was still an English colony, much of the eastern forests were logged for English ship building and lumber trade. White oaks were prized due to their resistance to rot and superior strength. In the book, *A Natural History of Trees*, by Donald Culross Peattie, the white oaks were directly referred to, *"The immortal frigate Constitution had a gun deck of solid White Oak of Massachusetts, her keel was the same wood from New Jersey, while knees of Maryland White Oak framed her keelsons."* Curved and unusually shaped trees would have been used because of their shape for things such as sawn frames, knees,

A view from atop the Highland Park bluffs overlooking Lake Michigan. Photo taken by the author.

This drawing of the "Old Oak" appeared in "The Story of Northwestern University," published in 1924.

This photo taken by the author shows the interesting Marker Tree that bears a resemblance to the "Old Oak" that stood at Northwestern University.

and stems (part of the bow) as discussed in an article *An Eye for Big Trees and Fine Boats* by Peggy Comfort. The author is a member of the Black Hawk Chapter of the Antique Boat Society and he contacted Jim Staib and Ted Cartner, both past presidents of the Chapter, to discuss this theory. Staib and Cartner referred Downes to Duke Besozzi, member of the Thoreau Society who works in sustainable white oak harvesting. During an interview, Besozzi confirmed that the practice of harvesting white oaks has gone on for centuries along the east coast and that the unusual shape of a Trail Marker Tree would have caught the eye of the harvester searching for specific shapes in the trees. Besozzi does not harvest any trees thought to be Trail Marker Trees, but confirmed the author's theory that they were harvested in the past.

Glencoe has a well-documented history with the Trail Marker Trees thanks to the efforts of its residents and social groups going back over 100 years.

Highland Park

Highland Park also has a well-documented history of their past Native American inhabitants. The Native Americans left many physical remains of their villages like stone artifacts, burial mounds, and the culturally modified trees. Some of these villages were high on the bluffs of the town overlooking Lake Michigan; one can only imagine what their name for this beautiful site might have been. In 1847, the area would take on the name St. John's Port. Not long after, in 1850, the name would be changed to Port Clinton. A famous fine art festival held every

year in Highland Park still honors the name and is called Port Clinton Fine Art Festival. This area is still well known for its beautiful bluffs, dramatic ravines, and gorgeous beach front. In 1869, the town of Port Clinton would become the city of Highland Park. Due to the foresight of the city planners, including Walter S. Gurnee, former mayor of Chicago, Highland Park would become developed as a residential area and great care was taken in the layout of the city. The city planners' hired famed landscape architects Horace W. S. Cleveland and William French to help ensure the beauty of the area was maintained. Another famous landscape architect, Jens Jensen, would later make Highland Park his home. Anyone who has walked through the ravines, up to the bluffs, and through the many other beautiful places in this old port town like Everett Millard Park, Central Park, Rosewood Park, and Sunset Woods Park could understand why people love to call Highland Park home.

The Highland Park area seemed to be a central hub or crossroads of many Indian trails. Some of these trails were part of the well-known Green Bay Trail along the shore of Lake Michigan. Many other trails lead away from Lake Michigan; one such trail led north west towards Mettawa, then to the Chain O'Lakes region, and on to Lake Geneva (in Wisconsin). Some of the most well-known Trail Marker Trees came from this area; many of these trees were studied by scholars, historians, and government agencies as early as the 1800's. These well-known Trail Marker Trees were also well documented. In the book *Pioneer to Commuter, The Story of Highland Park*,

by Marvyn Wittelle, the many trails and Trail Marker Trees are directly referred to: *"Highland Park was a portion of the, "Illinois Country" annexed to the French province of Louisiana. Joliet's mission ushered in a lustrous era of fur trade, French forts and war. Key trails to trading posts at Detroit and Green Bay, Wisconsin were marked by saplings which the Indians fastened to the ground—one route forded the Skokies, another paralleled the lakefront from Fort Dearborn to Waukeganence, a fort allegedly founded in 1695 by the French explorer La Salle."*

Another well documented part of Highland Park history is the Indian Village that was located on the bluffs near the McGregor Adams and Sylvester Millard estates. Author Julia Johnas of Highland Park verified that both the Millard and McGregor Adams estates were very large estates located along the lake front where the Indian Village was located. Sylvester Millard was born in 1839 and passed away in 1905. During his lifetime, he was deeply involved in the city's early days. His son, Everett Lee Millard, was born in 1877 and was raised at what is referred to as "The Log House" built in the 1840's and still standing as a historical landmark today. Everett grew up playing and hiking on the ancient Indian sites surrounding his home. When it came time for college, Everett attended Harvard University and then went on to law school at Northwestern University, where he graduated. While still attending college, Everett and a fellow classmate, Vernon Cassard, conceived the idea for the Exmoor Country Club. They gained financial support of William A. Alexander,

who purchased the land and funded the building of the clubhouse. Mr. Alexander would become the first president of the Exmoor Country Club. The Exmoor, a known site of Indian Trail Marker Trees, would open its doors in 1896. Its land has been beautifully preserved even to date; parts of the original forest on its property have been saved from being cut down.

Later in life, as an attorney, Everett Millard and E.L. Ryerson would attempt the first passage of the Lake County Forest Preserve Act. Decades later, it would finally be put into law. Everett became appointed chairman of the city of Highland Park Beautification Program, and throughout his life, he was a man who fought for nature.

The remains of the Indian Village near the Everett property included the rare structural remains of a council house. This circular council house was 30 feet in diameter and had a raised mound in the interior. Since the structure of the house was created and shaped from local, rot resistant, hardwood trees, it could be seen for decades after the Native Americans had left the area. In 1905, C.S. Raddin, of the Chicago Academy of Sciences, gave a description of this Council House and stated that there were trails leading to and from this house marked by Trail Marker Trees. That same year, Frank R. Grover, submitted a paper to the Chicago Historical Society, giving a similar description of the site. Another well-known Indian Village site, located in Chicago, became an attraction during the 1893 World's Fair.

pages 86–87
This photo of the "Old Oak" was taken in the late 1800's showing Northwestern University's Class of 1880. This enormous oak, at the time 250 years old, would have served as a marker along the shore of Lake Michigan.

Photograph of the plaque dedicated to honor Everett Millard for his many contributions to maintaining Highland Park's natural beauty.

This photograph shows the Marker Tree that was discussed by Janssen in the article Living Guide Posts of the Past, this unusual Marker Tree is still standing today.

This photograph shows another example of the unusually shaped Marker Trees that were discussed by Janssen; this tree was also in Highland Park. Photo courtesy of Highland Park Historical Society.

This photo, taken by the author, shows the same unusual Marker Tree nearly seventy years later.

This photo taken in the 1950's shows the Trail Marker Tree that was located on Hazel Avenue, one of the most well-known and photographed Trail Marker Trees. By the 1950's the main trunk of this tree had broken and it had fallen into the ground. Photo courtesy of the Lake County Museum Archives.

Highland Park is located just north of Glencoe along the shoreline. The special form of Trail Marker Tree that was seen near the Green Bay Trail in Glencoe is also seen near the Green Bay Trail in Highland Park. One of these trees was documented and photographed a century ago and is still standing today. This Trail Marker Tree is located in southern Highland Park, but the exact location cannot be disclosed because it is standing on private property. Local horticulturalist, Nadean Buchholz, informed Dennis about this tree and arranged a meeting between the property owners and the author. The property owners were pleased to meet with the author and learned that this tree had been photographed and mentioned in several articles in the past. In the article, *Living Guide Posts of the Past*, Raymond Janssen wrote, *"This white oak was bent quite high from the ground (about seven feet) and marks the intersection of two former Indian trails. Other bent trees along these trails are still standing at various distances in the four directions from it. It is located in Highland Park, Illinois."*

Another documented example comes from the 1929 *Arnold Arboretum New York*, published by Harvard University. This book discusses the 11 Trail Marker Trees that were known to be in perfect alignment, leading from the Indian Village (mentioned above) in a northwesterly direction for many miles. All of the trees in this particular line were white oak. One of the Trail Marker Trees from the line of 11 stood on Hazel Avenue in Highland Park; this tree appeared in the

book *Trees: Yearbook of Agriculture*, published in 1949 by the United States Department of Agriculture. This book included a sketch and a short explanation about the Trail Marker Trees, as well as an acknowledgement of the Daughters of the American Revolution for their work on saving the trees. This same tree on Hazel Avenue also appeared in the 1955 *World Book Encyclopedia*. Downes was made aware of this particular reference by Tony Weaks from South Carolina, with whom Downes has been working with in that region of the country. Later the author was able to locate the reference with the help of Neal Samors, Ph.D. who had a copy of this edition of the *World Book* in his library. The appearance of Trail Marker Trees in major publications like this helped to raise awareness across the country, resulting in many Trail Marker Trees being saved and preserved that might otherwise have been lost.

Two other well-known Trail Marker Trees in the Highland Park area were located on the grounds of the Exmoor Country Club. The Exmoor Country Club was built on land that was ceded from the Potawatomi in 1833, and its doors were opened in 1896. The club maintained strong ties with its community during both World Wars by opening its doors to the troops, offering both lodging and entertainment. Also in 1918, during the Influenza Epidemic, the Exmoor Country Club opened its doors again and served as a hospital, staffed by its members and employees, saving countless lives. In the late 1980s the author became aware of one of the Trail Marker Trees that stood on the grounds of the Exmoor Country Club.

A historian of the Lakes Region Historical Society in Antioch gave Dennis a photograph of the Trail Marker Tree and informed him that it was no longer standing as it had died years ago. Since the tree no longer existed, Dennis decided he did not need to visit the site and filed the information in his Highland Park file. As fate would have it, the author would go to the Exmoor Country Club years later on a snowy night in December of 2002; he drove to the Exmoor to meet his girlfriend Gail (now wife) at the Curling Club Christmas Party. When Dennis arrived at the Country Club, he was greeted by member Michael Griem. Mr. Griem recognized Dennis from the newspaper, as he had been in many articles relating to the Trail Marker Trees. Mr. Griem then took the author outside through the snow behind the club house. With a broom, Mr. Griem brushed off a large boulder that had a bronze plaque attached to it; this boulder and plaque had been placed next to the Trail Marker Tree in the 1930s, while it was still standing. The plaque was made and placed by the Exmoor Country Club with the help of local historians and was inscribed: *"This bur oak is a Pottawatomie Indian Trail Tree marking a trail extending North-West from Lake Michigan through these grounds. The Trail Marker was bent in this shape while a young sapling more than a hundred and fifty years ago. 1935."* This Trail Marker Tree is located just off of the Green Bay Trail that ran through the area.

Mr. Griem attended several Trail Marker Tree exhibits in the following years. After talking to other members of the

This photograph shows the traditional Trail Marker Tree that stood behind the Exmoor Clubhouse and the boulder on which the commemorative plaque for the tree was placed. This photo was taken by Hazel Avery in 1957. Photo courtesy of the Lake County Museum Archives.

The author's wife, Gail, preparing for the National Curling Championships. Gail was the first woman president of the Illinois Curling Association.

On a return trip to the Exmoor Country Club, the author and Greg Prochnow searched the golf course and surrounding woodland areas. This tree is an example of some of the old growth trees that still stand in the area. Photo taken by the author.

This photo shows the actual boulder and plaque that were originally shown to Downes by Mr. Griem on his first visit to the Exmoor Country Club. This photo was taken on the author's return trip to the grounds of the Exmoor Country Club.

This White Oak Trail Marker Tree stood in Highland Park east of Green Bay Road. Photo courtesy of Ainsley Brook Wonderling, Museum Director, Lakes Region Historical Society.

The author standing by the entrance to Sunset Woods Park; this park had a traditional Trail Marker Tree verified by Ron Bernardi.

Dennis standing in front of the Highland Park Historical Society.

Club, Mr. Griem informed the author about another Trail Marker Tree that had stood on the grounds of Exmoor. Unfortunately this tree had also passed away years earlier. But with this reference, Dennis was able to find more information to support this fact. In the book, *A History of Lake County Illinois*, by John Halsey in 1912, it is stated that there were in fact two Trail Marker Trees standing on the grounds of the Exmoor Country Club. Later the author also located a photograph of this second Trail Marker Tree in an article by Raymond Janssen titled *Living Guide Posts of the Past*. These two trees were preserved for years by the members of the Exmoor Country Club who were aware of their significance and passed away only due to natural causes. Through the combined efforts of the Exmoor and local historians, thousands of visitors to the club were able to see these trees and later the commemorative plaque that still remains today, continuing to raise awareness of the significance of these Native American historical landmarks.

Another area of Highland Park that is known to have had a Trail Marker Tree is Sunset Woods Park, also known as Sheahen Woods. The author first had this park brought to his attention by Daniel English. Mr. English informed Downes about several culturally modified trees in the area. Downes is still investigating the significance. However, while studying the area, the author remembered another reference to Sunset Woods he had heard much earlier. Ron Bernardi, who lived near the park in the 1940s, told the author about a Trail Marker Tree that stood in the park while he was a child. Mr. Bernardi remembers this tree was located on the east side of the park and remembers playing on it as a child. Mr. Bernardi confirmed that this Trail Marker Tree was a traditional oak Trail Marker Tree.

During Dennis' research in Highland Park, he was able to locate information about many alternate uses that the Europeans had for the Trail Marker Trees. Jobe Cerny of the Highland Park Historical Society was very helpful to Downes' research and referred him to Nancy Webster, the Historical Society's archivist. Nancy Webster helped Downes to locate many articles, including an article, *Those Crooked Trees*, written by John A. Peters who wrote for the Historical Society in the early 1900s. The article discussed that the Trail Marker Trees were sought after by shipbuilders and furniture builders for their specific curved shape, or "knees." Peters even referenced that full car loads of these trees were shipped on the railroads to sawmills. Another use that Peters discussed was using the Trail Marker Trees as "stone boats." The Trail Marker Trees would be cut in half lengthwise, positioned about six feet apart, and connected with supports making a sled that could be used to haul rocks or firewood easily in the winter months, most often used by farmers. This practice was well known and even mentioned to the author by his father-in-law, Dr. Elroy Spreen, in Medford, Wisconsin. These practices unfortunately led to the demise of countless Trail Marker Trees not only in this area but in many other areas of the country as well.

The Highland Park area preserved many Trail Marker Trees with the help of several groups of concerned citizens. Through their efforts, the knowledge and awareness of these Native American landmarks has been increased not only in their area but across the country.

Deerfield

The village of Deerfield was first settled in 1835 by Horace Lamb and Jacob Cadwell; its first name was Cadwell's Corner. Before its first European settlers, Deerfield was known for its Potawatomi Indian population. The area's navigable rivers, the Des Plaines River and Chicago River, along with its vast deer populations, made it a desirable place and it began to grow quickly. By the 1850s it took on the name Deerfield, and by 1903, the village became incorporated. Today Deerfield is known for its many beautiful and well-kept parks.

One of Deerfield's parks is the location of a living double trunk Trail Marker Tree that was documented in the 1930's by Raymond Janssen; this park bears the name Trail Tree Park. Although trees from the oak family were most commonly used in this area, this Trail Marker Tree is a maple tree. Over the years the village has made an effort to watch over and protect the tree. They have even installed a fence around the tree to ensure it is not damaged. This ancient Trail Marker Tree's base has expanded greatly over the last century; a distortion that is common amongst the oldest Trail Marker Trees. Several years

This photo, taken by the author, shows the enormous upright limbs of this double trunk Trail Marker Tree.

This photograph of the Deerfield Trail Marker Tree was part of the Bess Dunn collection. Photo courtesy of the Lake County Museum.

This photo is a close up of the informational sign the Village of Deerfield created with the help of the author to help educate park visitors about the Trail Marker Trees.

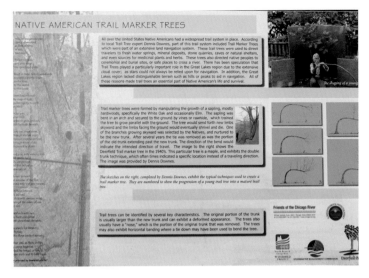

ago, the village contacted the author to assist them in creating a permanent informational sign that was to be installed near the Trail Marker Tree. This sign explains the significance of the Trail Marker Trees, how to identify key characteristics, and even how they were shaped including sketches from the author and a photograph of one of his Trail Marker Trees. The Trail Marker Tree and informational sign can be seen in the park today.

Another traditional Trail Marker Tree that was documented in Deerfield was photographed nearly 100 years ago by Bess Dunn. This tree stood on the west side of Deerfield, but is no longer standing today. Dennis grew up in the area, canoeing many of the lakes and rivers, and has revisited the area over the years to study the land in the western part of Deerfield. He believes that this Trail Marker Tree and others would have guided the Native Americans to a river crossing over the Des Plaines River. This specific trail, running between Deerfield and Northbrook, would have followed what is now Dundee Road, coming from the west and leading towards Lake Michigan. Thanks to the efforts of the village of Deerfield and its residents, one of these ancient Native American landmarks can still be seen.

Lincolnshire

The village of Lincolnshire is located just northwest of Deerfield and was not incorporated until 1957; it was originally part of Half Day. This area was known for being one of the

This photograph was taken in the Florsheim Preserve and shows the author and Alex standing by the double trunk Trail Marker Tree.

This photograph is from the 1941 article in *The Scientific Monthly* and shows the same double trunk Trail Marker Tree nearly 70 years earlier.

Potawatomi Village sites along the Des Plaines River. The first Europeans known to visit this area were the French Jesuit explorers, including Father Jacques Marquette and Louis Joliet. They arrived in the area in 1673, at what is now Waukegan ('Little Fort'), and traveled down the Des Plaines River coming into contact with the Potawatomi Indians of the area. The first European settler in this region was Captain Daniel Wright, who came to the area in 1834. Captain Wright was granted permission by the Potawatomi Chief Halfda to build his cabin at the south end of the Potawatomi village; presently the site is the intersection of Milwaukee Avenue and Aptakisic Road.

The author is very familiar with this area, living just off of Milwaukee Avenue and Aptakisic Road on the Des Plaines River for two years in the 1970s. Dennis moved to this area after living at The Grove in the early '70s. During the years he lived here, Dennis and his lifelong friend, Tom English, kayaked the Des Plaines River in a kayak built by Tom's father. Years later in 2007, Dennis would return to the area at the request of a local family. A young boy named Alex, with the help of his mother, sent a letter to the author's home; Alex had taken an interest in what he thought were Trail Marker Trees in his local forest preserve. Upon receiving the letter, Dennis contacted Alex's mother and agreed to drive down and meet Alex and see his possible Trail Marker Trees. These trees are located in Florsheim Nature Preserve in Lincolnshire. The Florsheim Nature Preserve is considered to be one of the jewels of the Lincolnshire area. The preserve is a rarity in its native

qualities. Thus it has a high Floristic Quality Index (FQI) rating of 82.01. This rating system was developed by the Morton Arboretum in Illinois as a means of determining the quality of a natural area based on numeric rating given to each plant species. One of the developers, Gerould Wilhelm, stated: *"Remnant areas with FQI values approaching 60 or higher are very rare, and occupy a minute fraction of the remaining vegetated land surface of our region."* With a FQI rating of 82.01, this preserve truly is exceptional and of value to the area.

When the author visited Alex and his mother, they all were able to hike through the beautiful Florsheim Preserve. Alex led the author to a tree that was a double trunk Trail Marker Tree; this tree resembled the Fuller Tree in Winnetka. After hiking further through the woods, the next tree they came across was a Marker Tree that resembles the "Pointer Tree" in Bristol, Wisconsin. Dennis photographed and documented both of these trees for his records. After his visit with Alex, Dennis located an old article from *The Scientific Monthly* that he had found years earlier. This article, written by Raymond Janssen in 1941, included a photo of the double trunk Trail Marker Tree the author had just seen in the Florsheim Preserve and now connected to this article. In this article Janssen wrote, *"There are numerous reasons to mark a trail, even though the general direction to be traveled is known. A direct route from one locality to another might be obstructed by natural barriers such as unusual elevations or depressions, non-fordable bodies of water, treacherous swamps or dense thickets of thorny*

underbrush. To facilitate travel, a marked detour might be advisable." Shortly after the author's trip to the Florsheim Preserve, Alex again contacted Downes. This time Alex was planning to complete a school project about Trail Marker Trees and was hoping for Downes' help. Dennis was able to provide photographs and more information to help Alex complete his project. Through this young boy's curiosity, the author was able to connect his old research to a living Trail Marker Tree and expand his study in the Lincolnshire area.

Mettawa

One of the earliest references to the Mettawa area by its current name was in 1833 in a diary now held by the Chicago History Museum (Chicago Historical Society). The first mayor of Mettawa was James R. Getz; he was known for his interest in local history. In 1955, Mr. Getz wrote a paper entitled, *Notes on the Indians of Lake County*, in which he mentions a study of the Trail Marker Trees conducted by Bess Dunn in the early 1900's. Mr. Getz was also the president of the Lake County Historical Society and involved himself with the study of the Trail Marker Trees.

The village of Mettawa boasts five forest preserves within their borders and is dedicated to preserving open lands. Linda and Fredrick Phillips live on Deerpath Farm, a large 200-acre parcel that was once owned by the famous architect Edward H. Bennett Senior and today is a conservation community that has helped to keep 140 acres preserved as open land.

Edward Bennett is known for his work with Daniel Burnham on the 1909 Plan of Chicago and is also one of the most famous former residents of Mettawa. Fredrick Phillips, Edward Bennett's great grandson, is currently the architect for Deerpath Farm. Linda is known locally as a historian and is very knowledgeable about the community's history. Originally the Mettawa area was inhabited by the Native Americans and had many Indian trails; remnants of some of these trails can still be seen today. These Indian trails led in many directions. One of the most prominent trails led from the Highland Park area, northwest through Mettawa, towards the Fox River Valley, and on to Lake Geneva. Today there are many nicely manicured trails through the acres of open lands used by hikers, equestrians, and nature enthusiasts.

Years ago, Dennis met Heidi Fornarotto during the Lake Forest Fine Art Show where he had his bronze Trail Marker Tree on display. Over the years, Heidi attended many more shows and Trail Marker Tree exhibits and became friends with the author. On one specific occasion, Heidi brought her son, Joe, and friend, Mike Baird, to Downes' studio where they discussed the Trail Marker Trees of the area. After this meeting, Mr. Baird spoke with Jess Ray (the mayor of Mettawa) about the author and the Trail Marker Trees. Mayor Ray contacted Downes in order to find out more information about the Trail Marker Trees in the area.

Dennis' friend, Heidi, owns several horses and has become very familiar with the many horse trails throughout the Mettawa

area. During her time spent riding these trails, Heidi discovered the location of a possible Trail Marker Tree and informed Dennis about it. With the help of Mayor Ray, the author was able to locate the property and document the Trail Marker Tree. The property on which this Trail Marker Tree stands is private property and the owners would prefer to keep their location private. However, during the author's visit, the owners were happy to help and talk with him about the tree. At the suggestion of Mayor Ray, Dennis also made a visit to the Merit Club (Golf Course), this property was once owned by the Getz Family. On the grounds of the club still stands a large oak tree, estimated to be over 300 years old. When the author visited the club, John Nelson, the superintendent, helped him to locate the tree. The Getz family protected and nurtured this tree for generations and created a plaque to be placed by the tree, denoting its significance in 1930. The sign has since been replaced with a newer version by the National Arborist Association. Today, the Getz Family owns property next to the club and they continue to care for the old oak.

During the author's research in Mettawa, he came across several young trees that appear to have been recently shaped to resemble Trail Marker Trees. In other areas where Trail Marker Trees were prevalent, Downes has noticed a similar trend. The author believes these trees were shaped by Trail Marker Tree enthusiasts who were hoping to replace Trail Marker Trees that have been lost.

Lake Forest

The city of Lake Forest is located directly along one of the most famous and oldest Native American trails, the Green Bay Trail, which connected Fort Dearborn (Chicago) to Fort Howard (Green Bay). Lake Forest is known for its natural beauty and its efforts to preserve open lands as well as historic landmarks. As with many of the other towns located along the Green Bay Trail, Lake Forest is known to have had many Trail Marker Trees in the area.

One of the first documented references to the Trail Marker Trees in the Lake Forest area was in 1838 in a federal survey. John J. Halsey LL.D., professor of Political Science at Lake Forest College, commented on this reference in his 1912 book, *A History of Lake County Illinois*. In his book, Halsey mentions several Trail Marker Trees in Lake County, including trees in Lake Forest. A giant cottonwood used as a Marker Tree was located on the edge of the Onwentsia Club. The Onwentsia Club opened in 1895 and remains a prestigious golf club today. One of the next documented references to a Trail Marker Tree in the Lake Forest area is a photograph taken in 1897 at Fort Sheridan. Fort Sheridan, a military base, is located just outside of Lake Forest along the shores of Lake Michigan. This photograph shows several Cavalry officers posing in front of the Trail Marker Tree that was located at Fort Sheridan. The Cavalry officers would have been aware of the value of these culturally altered natural landmarks; they would have used them as reference

This photograph, taken by the author, shows the sign placed near the ancient oak.

Downes next to the Trail Marker Tree located on private property in Mettawa.

This photograph taken on the Deerpath Farm, shows a newly shaped tree, most likely shaped by a Trail Marker Tree enthusiast.

This photograph taken by Downes while on a research trip in Mettawa shows brilliantly colored fungus growing on a dead fall.

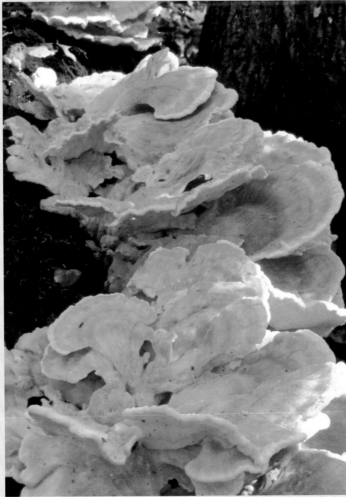

points much like the Native Americans did. The officers shown in this photograph are Maj. C.D. Viele, Capt. R.P.P. Wainwright, 1st Lieut. M.E. Davis, 2nd Lieut. R.C. Williams, and 2nd Lieut. W.M. Whitman. These officers were all accomplished Cavalry men. A personal friend of the author's, William Gleespen, was a military technician and had been stationed at Fort Sheridan. He helped Downes confirm the location of the tree on the base, which would have been near the barracks. Recently, a second photograph that showed the same tree was discovered by the author's assistant; this photograph verified Mr. Gleespen's opinion of the actual location of this historic landmark.

Another Lake Forest Trail Marker Tree was photographed by Bess Dunn during her study of the trees in the early 1900's. This Trail Marker Tree was located west of Waukegan Road, just off of Everett Road in west Lake Forest. This photograph was kept in a collection by the Lake County Historical Society. James Getz, former president of the Lake County Historical Society, sent some of Bess Dunn's photos to neighboring historical societies to help educate the public about the Trail Marker Trees. The Getz family has always advocated the importance of local history; their contributions led to the Special Collections and Archives section at the Lake Forest College Library. Later in 1934, a photograph of this same tree was included in an article, *Indian Trail Trees*, by Raymond Janssen. This Directional Trail Marker Tree was the author's inspiration

previous page
This photograph taken in 1897 shows the Officers of the Cavalry Squadron standing in front of the Directional Trail Marker Tree on the grounds of Fort Sheridan. Ainsley Wonderling of the Lakes Region Historical Society brought this photograph to the author's attention. Photo courtesy of the Lake County Discovery Museum, Lake County History Archives.

This photograph shows the Trail Marker Tree that stood on the grounds of Fort Sheridan near the barracks. This photograph was taken shortly after the 1897 Cavalry photograph. Photo courtesy of the Lake County Discovery Museum, Lake County History Archives.

This photograph of a Lake Forest Trail Marker Tree was part of Bess Dunn's photographic collection. Photo courtesy of the Lake County Museum Archives.

The author's wife next to his Trail Marker Tree exhibit at the Lake Forest Art Expo. Dennis participated in this event presented by the Women's Board of Catholic Charities for over a decade, as well as the Gala of the Arts that helped to support the Catholic Charities Emergency Assistance Program. Over the years, Peggy and Sam Ciccarelli helped give the author

the opportunity to present his Trail Marker Tree exhibit at many of these events

The author standing by his bronze Trail Marker Tree at the LEAD fundraiser. Downes was asked to participate in this event by Adrian and Nancy Smith, Lake Forest residents. The LEAD group is dedicated to the promotion of healthy families and the prevention of youth substance abuse and other risky behavior.

Raymond Janssen standing next to the Lake Forest Trail Marker Tree nearly three decades after Bess Dunn photographed this same tree. This photograph appeared in Janssen's 1934 article, Indian Trail Trees.

This photograph appeared in a *News-Sun* article in 1936. These two women, Mrs. C. D. Shipley and Mrs. Paul LaRose (left to right) were members of the DAR involved with the dedication ceremony for one of the Lake Bluff Trail Marker Trees. They also were in-volved with the dedication ceremonies for trees in Zion and Round Lake. Photo courtesy of Valerie L. Voyer Perron of the Little Fort Chapter, DAR.

The author and Lake Forest artist Franklin McMahon at the Aid for Women Fundraiser held at the Conrad Hilton in Chicago.

for his first bronze sculpture of a Trail Marker Tree in the early 1990s.

Downes has many ties to Lake Forest. He is a member of the Deer Path Art League and has been involved with the Lake Forest Art Expo (presented by the Women's Board of Catholic Charities of Lake County), the Lake Forest Fine Art Show, and other fundraising events. The author's participation in these events allowed him to display his written, photographic, and sculptural Trail Marker Tree exhibit to thousands of people over 20 years. At the Lake Forest Art Expo, Downes was privileged to exhibit with Franklin McMahon, known as *"The Man Who Draws History."* McMahon understood the concept of the Trail Marker Trees and commended Downes' work. Encouraging words from great individuals such as McMahon helped inspire the author throughout his continued research.

Lake Bluff

The Village of Lake Bluff was incorporated in 1895. However, some of its earliest residents settled the area in 1836. Early residents William and Mary Dwyer opened a stage coach stop along the Green Bay Trail. For many years Lake Bluff was a resort town frequented by Chicagoans because of its beautiful beaches, bluffs, and ravines. Today, the village encourages a healthy and natural environment through their Village Tree Management Program, and they have been awarded the "Tree City USA" award year after year for their efforts.

This photograph of Bess Dunn and the Lake Bluff Trail Marker Tree is the same photograph used in the 1910 postcard. Photo courtesy of the Lake County Museum Archives.

Nearly a century later, the author is shown next to this ancient Trail Marker Tree in Beulah Park. Over the years, this enormous tree has changed very little, its dimensions have barely changed and it has only lost one of its upright limbs. Photo taken by Greg Prochnow.

This photograph taken circa the late 1800's shows the Trail Marker Tree that is still standing today in Beulah Park, Zion, Illinois. Photo courtesy of Ainsley Brook Wonderling, Museum Director, Lakes Region Historical Society.

Lake Bluff also has a well-documented history with the Trail Marker Trees. There are two well-known Trail Marker Trees in the area and references to others as well. The earliest documentation of a Lake Bluff Trail Marker Tree was circa 1910; a photograph from Bess Dunn's photographic study of the Trail Marker Trees was made into a postcard. This photograph showed Bess Dunn standing in the bend of this Trail Marker Tree. This tree was a specific type of Trail Marker Tree commonly seen in the North Shore area and explained by Raymond Janssen in his article *Living Guide Posts of the Past*, as discussed earlier in this chapter. This photograph was also featured in the magazine *Natural History* 1940 and in the book *This Land of Lakes and Rivers: an Illustrated History of Lake County*, by Virginia Mullery. This Trail Marker Tree stood on Scranton Avenue until the 1940s.

During the course of the author's study regarding the involvement of the Daughters of the American Revolution with the Trail Marker Trees, Regent of the Fort Dearborn Chapter, Edith Trutter Hauff recommended that he contact Valerie L. Voyer Perron, past Regent of the Little Fort Chapter. Through this connection, Downes was able to locate information about the other well-documented Trail Marker Tree in Lake Bluff. Valerie L. Voyer Perron provided the author with copies of articles, minutes from the D.A.R. meetings, and other materials. This more traditional Trail Marker Tree stood at 525 North Avenue. The Waukegan Chapter (now called the Little Fort Chapter) of the D.A.R., with the help of the Lake

This photograph taken in 1935 depicts a local interested in the Trail Marker Trees that had just taken a taxi to visit this Trail Marker Tree site. Photo courtesy of the Lake County Museum Archives.

This Marker Tree was said to have stood just off of Telegraph Road near North Chicago, once referred to as Five Points. Photo courtesy of Ainsley Brook Wonderling, Museum Director, Lakes Region Historical Society.

Potawatomi Historical Expert, Knonozo, stands in the center of the sacred circle where the annual Potawatomi Powwow is held at Shiloh Park. Photo taken by the author.

Bluff Women's Club, had a dedication ceremony for this Trail Marker Tree in 1936. The D.A.R. had a bronze tablet in a boulder placed beside the historic landmark during the dedication ceremony that was attended by nearly 100 school children, Boy and Girl Scouts, Garden Club members, and other village organizations. This Trail Marker Tree remained standing until the 1960's when it fell due to disease. This tree and the tree located on Scranton Avenue were both documented in the book *Postcard History Series, Lake Bluff* by Lyndon Jensen and Kathleen O'Hara.

Another documented Trail Marker Tree stood near by a spring on the grounds of what is now the Shore Acres Golf Club. This Trail Marker Tree was said to be another of the specially formed Trail Marker Trees explained by Raymond Janssen. This tree was written about in 1935 by Mr. Horton of Lake County. The photographic documentation, postcards, and special ceremonies endeared the Trail Marker Trees of the area to the local residents.

Waukegan and Surrounding Areas

The French explorers Louis Joliet and Jacques Marquette were given credit as becoming Waukegan's first European visitors in 1673. In the book, *Pioneer to Commuter, The Story of Highland Park*, Marvyn Wittelle discusses an Indian trail marked by shaped saplings that led from Fort Dearborn to Waukeganence, which was said to be a fort founded by LaSalle in 1695. Waukegan is one of the oldest communities in Illinois. In its

early days it was named "Little Fort." In 1849, the community no longer wanted to be characterized by the term "Little" and voted to change their name to Waukegan, the Indian word for fort. Waukegan was incorporated as a city in 1859.

One of the most famous Trail Marker Trees in the Waukegan area is still standing in Beulah Park, north of Waukegan in Zion. This tree was initially documented in the late 1800's or early 1900s by Bess Dunn during her photographic study. Bess Bower Dunn was the head of the Lake County Historical Society and when she died, she was eulogized as having done more for the preservation of history in Lake County than any other individual. After Bess Dunn's study, in the 1930's the Waukegan Chapter D.A.R. (now called the Little Fort Chapter) held a dedication ceremony to honor this Trail Marker Tree. This ancient oak Trail Marker Tree sits on the upper edge of a ravine and has been documented to mark the way to a nearby chipping station where the Native Americans would have worked with stone and minerals to make tools, weapons, and adornments. During the first dedication ceremony in 1936, the Waukegan Chapter D.A.R. had a bronze tablet in a granite block placed near the tree to educate all who read it about this historic tree and its purpose. Decades later, in 1995, the Potawatomi Trail Marker Tree was designated a city landmark by the Zion City Council. In July 1995 a special Native American re-dedication ceremony was held in honor of the tree. Years later, in 2001, the Little Fort Chapter DAR and the Potawatomi Indians held another

re-dedication celebration for this remaining Trail Marker Tree. Many tribal elders and other tribal members attended this celebration from the Forest County Potawatomi Reservation. Downes' research led him to this tree in the late 1960s; he has visited and photographed the tree on several occasions. In more recent years the author has attended the annual Potawatomi Powwow that is held at the nearby Shiloh Park. Shiloh Park is another historically significant park with many ties to its Native American Past. Downes was able to meet Potawatomi historical expert, Knonozo (Steve Young), at Shiloh Park. They discussed the nearby Trail Marker Tree at Beulah Park along with effigy mounds, other Trail Marker Trees, and burial mounds located throughout northeastern Illinois and southeastern Wisconsin.

Another documented tree in the Waukegan area stood west of Route 41 and south of Washington Street, near what today is Park City. This classic example of a Directional Trail Marker Tree is no longer standing but has been documented through photographs from the early 1900's. Another tree that has long since fallen once stood in the Oakwood Cemetery near the edge of the ravine, located near Lake Michigan off of Sheridan Road. This tree was referred to in Mr. Horton's paper, *Indian Trail Trees in Lake County*, 1935. Mr. Horton believed this tree led to the known Indian burial ground southeast of the cemetery. A non-traditional documented Marker Tree from the Waukegan area was located along Waukegan Road west of North Chicago. This tree was part of Bess Dunn's

photographic study in the early 1900's. Downes has documented other similar Marker Trees in several other states and has found historical references to them as candelabra trees. These trees most often have been used to mark boundaries or show areas of portage. The author believes Waukegan's location along the historic Green Bay Trail led to more public awareness of the Trail Marker Trees. Through the efforts of local historians, the D.A.R., and Native Americans, groups the trees in the Waukegan area have been documented and not forgotten.

Antioch and the Chain O'Lakes Region

Before the arrival of the European settlers, the Chain O'Lakes region was a pristine area of lakes, rivers, streams, rolling hills, and dense forests. Today, it is known that Lake County has nearly 200 lakes and ponds in addition to the numerous rivers, streams, and creeks. Very few places could rival this region's abundance of natural resources including the fresh water, wild game, fish, water fowl, wild rice, and vast varieties of edible plants. The rivers were full of mussels that provided food and ornamental adornments. The wide variety of birds and water fowl that migrated through the area also provided both food and feathers for adornments. Many Native American Tribes maintained control of the Chain O'Lakes region throughout history, but the Potawatomi were the last Indian tribe to have control of the land before it was ceded to the American government. This area was well traveled and had many trails leading all directions across the land.

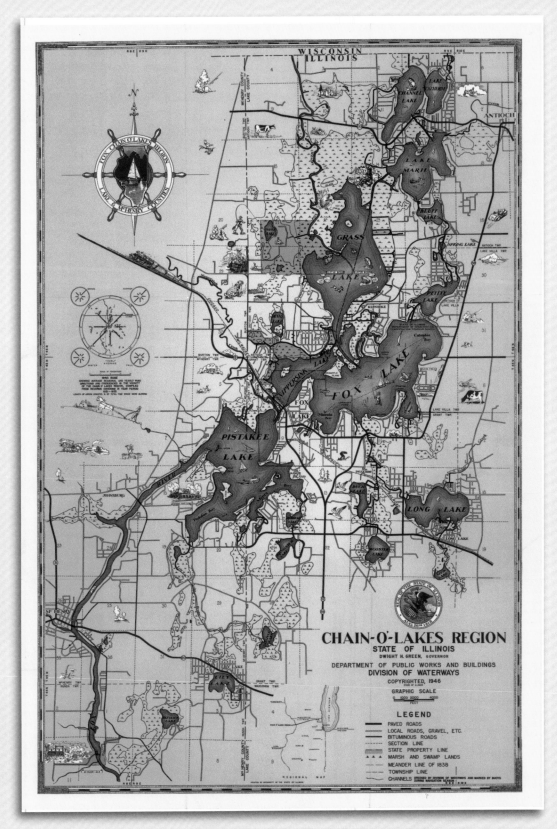

CHAIN-O'-LAKES REGION
STATE OF ILLINOIS
DWIGHT H. GREEN, GOVERNOR
DEPARTMENT OF PUBLIC WORKS AND BUILDINGS
DIVISION OF WATERWAYS
COPYRIGHTED, 1946

View of Chas. F. Haling's Resort from Boat Landing,
Hunters and Fishermens' Headquarters on Grass Lake, Antioch, Ill. 670

This postcard from the early 1900's shows the famous Egyptian Lotus Beds of Grass Lake and the viewing tower for tourists at Blarney's Island. Beginning in the late 1800's this was a tourist destination for many Midwesterners. Photo courtesy of Ainsley Brook Wonderling, Museum Director, Lakes Region Historical Society.

This postcard from the early 1900's shows the Haling's Resort circa 1900 located on Grass Lake. This family run Marina is still operated by the Haling Family today. Photo courtesy of Ainsley Brook Wonderling, Museum Director, Lakes Region Historical Society.

This aerial view of the Chain O'Lakes Region was taken by the author while flying over the area with Dr. Harry Spell and his wife Karly of Art Casting of Illinois.

The Lakes Region Historical Society located in Antioch, Illinois. This Historical Society helped the author with some of his earliest research on the Trail Marker Trees of the area.

The Great Blue Heron at home in the back waters of the Chain O'Lakes Region. Photo taken by the author.

Some of these trails would lead to the many areas of special interest to the Native Americans, including areas of medicinal plants, safe portage, and areas of exposed mineral deposits. One trail led west out of the area towards Galena where there were known lead deposits then onward to the Mississippi River. Some of these main Indian trails would become stagecoach routes and much later they would be turned into highways. In the town of Wilmot, just northwest of Antioch, an old hotel that served as a rest stop for weary stagecoach travelers still stands today. The Wilmot Hotel, founded in 1848, is now called the Stage Stop, the oldest tap and dining establishment in Wisconsin. Today, the Chain O'Lakes region is known as an outdoor recreation area where residents and visitors alike can enjoy fishing, boating, hiking, and horseback riding trails.

Downes has lived in the Chain O'Lakes region for 30 years. He moved to the area in the early 1980s on the northern side of Fox Lake, near Captain's Quarters Marina. After five years, Downes moved further north onto Channel Lake in Antioch. The village of Antioch maintains a historic home town feel and is known for its Native American history. Two of the main highways in the village, Highway 83 and Highway 173, were both known Indian trails. Although the author spends much of his time traveling in order to conduct research, his home remains on Channel Lake today. Even as a child, Dennis had ties to this area from his summer visits to his grandfather on Cedar Island located on Pistakee Lake.

One of the earliest references to a Trail Marker Tree in the Antioch was in 1852; a sketch of a Trail Marker Tree appeared on an official surveyor's report. The surveyor, George Hale resided in Antioch and was the elected surveyor of Lake County. Upon the sketch of the Trail Marker Tree the initials E.S.I. were shown; Ainsley Wonderling of the Lakes Region Historical Society was able to identify the initials as one of the earliest settlers in the region, Eleazar Stillman Ingalls. The author became aware of this survey from local resident and Native American history enthusiast, Mr. Roe. Historian, Ainsley Wonderling, believes this Trail Marker Tree was part of a line that led to Hackberry Island, which was a known campsite for the Native Americans located just off of the Fox River. The author has received hundreds of books through the Antioch Public Library using the interlibrary loan system with the help of Amy Blue, head of the Reference Department. These books, many of which are from the 1800s and earlier, have provided valuable information for the Trail Marker Tree study in this and other areas.

Nearby in Fox Lake, there are two documented Trail Marker Trees. The first documented Trail Marker Tree in Fox Lake was from a photographic study in the early 1900s. This Double Trunk Trail Marker Tree was located on Grand Avenue overlooking the lake. Another traditional Trail Marker Tree that stood near Fox Lake was documented by Raymond Janssen in his article *Living Guide Posts of the Past*, appearing in *Scientific Monthly*, 1941.

Dennis and part of the Sieben family holding an arrowhead found on the property by Sue Sieben. The Sieben's have had a cottage on Cedar Island since before Dennis was born.

Dennis (center) and his brothers, Lou (left) and Harry (right), as children visiting their grandfather on Cedar Island.

This photograph taken by the author from his deck shows the scenic beauty of the Chain O'Lakes Region.

This photograph shows the Double Trunk Trail Marker Tree on Grand Avenue in Fox Lake. Photo courtesy of the Lake County Museum Archives.

Raymond Janssen standing next to a Traditional Trail Marker Tree in Fox Lake in the Chain O'Lakes Region. This photo appeared in his article in *Scientific Monthly* in 1941.

A copy of Mr. George Hale's survey, 1852. Courtesy of the Lake County Recorder.

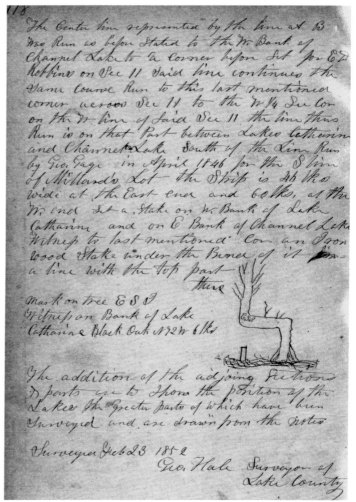

Just outside of the Chain O'Lakes region in the neighboring town of Round Lake there are several references to the Trail Marker Trees that once stood in the area. A Trail Marker Tree that stood on the Renehan Resort was photographed and turned into a postcard in the early 1900's. Later in the 1930s, with the help of Bess Dunn, the D.A.R. identified this tree and created a bronze tablet to honor this Trail Marker Tree. Two special Trail Marker Trees located on the grounds of the old Shorewood Golf Course, were very close together. These deliberately shaped trees were part of Bess Dunn's photographic study in the early 1900s and were also referenced in the *Images of America; Grayslake and Avon Township* by Charlotte K. Renehan, a local historian. Today, very near to where these trees were said to be located, a road is fittingly named, Indian Trail Road. Just west of where these two unique Trail Marker Trees were located another traditional Trail Marker Tree was located just off Highway 134 and West Long Lake Road. The author's friend, Bryan White, attended his first Trail Marker Tree Exhibit a decade ago and recognized the Trail Marker Trees. Bryan told Dennis that a similar tree was in the neighborhood where he grew up and gave Dennis the location of where the tree used to be located. With the help of Greg Prochnow, Dennis was able to find this Trail Marker Tree, photograph, and document it before it was removed a few years later.

Just west of the Chain O'Lakes region in the town of Hebron is located a Marker Tree that has received much attention

This photograph from the Bess Dunn photographic study in the early 1900's depicts two Trail Marker Trees side by side. Photo courtesy of the Lake County Museum Archives.

Dennis with Potawatomi historical expert, Steve Young, at the author's studio.

The author examines the Trail Marker Tree in Round Lake, this tree has since been taken down. Photo taken by Greg Prochnow.

An example of a Trail Marker Tree shaped by the author in the Chain O'Lakes Region. Photo taken by the author's assistant, Liz Fox.

from the locals. The author's cousins, Mike and Velma Downes, mailed Dennis a copy of the newsletter, *Field Notes*, put out by the Land Conservancy of McHenry County. In this newsletter, there was an article about an ancient bur oak that the locals had started calling the Spirit Tree; Mike and Velma knew that their cousin would want to research this further. This Marker Tree is located in the High Point Conservation Area and the author was able to contact Rich Dankert, site steward. Downes and his assistant, Liz Fox, met with Rich and he took them out to see the ancient bur oak Marker Tree. The author was able to photograph and document this tree and talk with Rich about his and the many locals' efforts to protect and conserve this Marker Tree.

The Chain O'Lakes region had many Trail Marker Trees, some of which were unfortunately not documented, but should not be forgotten. Based on several interviews with Steve Young, Potawatomi historical expert and local historian, the author was able to confirm that there were numerous Trail Marker Trees throughout this region and that the Trail Marker Tree system was firmly in place. Regrettably, due to the immense highway expansion and a lack of knowledge and understanding about the trees and their significance, many of these historical landmarks were lost over the past several decades.

Central Illinois and Areas along the Illinois River
Central Illinois is known as the Heart of Illinois and consists mostly of flat prairie lands. Centuries ago, these prairies would have provided endless grazing to the vast buffalo herds. However, along its northern border lay several state parks known for their breathtaking views from canyons, bluffs, and rock formations. Starved Rock State Park claims to be the most beautiful place in Illinois and is known for its Native American History.

Peoria is one of the oldest settlements in Illinois, primarily due to its location along the Illinois River; French explorers came to the area as early as 1680. Shortly after the author's four-month exhibit of the Trail Marker Tree sculpture at the Wildlife Prairie State Park in Peoria, a local resident contacted Downes about a Marker Tree just outside of Peoria near the town of Morton. The local resident, Byron Schrock, had lived in the area his entire life and his family had resided in the area for generations. Mr. Schrock was only nine years old when his grandfather showed and told him about an ancient Indian Marker Tree on their property that pointed to a nearby river.

This massive Marker Tree is still standing on the property today and Mr. Schrock, now in his 80s, told the author that the tree has barely changed in the nearly 70 years from the first time he saw it. Downes was able to meet Mr. Schrock and see this ancient Indian Marker Tree to photograph, measure, and document it.

Another local family that had seen the author's Trail Marker Tree sculpture at the Wildlife Prairie State Park sent him a letter with information about a Marker Tree

The famed Starved Rock. Photo taken by the author during one of his research trips.

This Trail Marker Tree located in Metamora has been partially buried due to construction and excavation above it on the ridge. This tree has been named 'Crooked Tree' by the Girl Scout Camp. Photo taken by Greg Prochnow.

The author and Byron Schrock standing upon this 400 year old sycamore Marker Tree.

Byron Schrock standing beneath the giant Marker Tree, its limb like an arm pointing to the nearby river.

on their property. This family unfortunately moved out of the area before the author was able to visit the site. However, the family did send Dennis photos and measurements of the tree.

Just northeast of Peoria in the town of Metamora is a well-known Trail Marker Tree located at a local Girl Scout camp. The author first heard about this tree during a Trail Marker Tree exhibit in downtown Chicago. This Trail Marker Tree has been used to teach the visiting Girl Scouts more about the local Native Americans and has been named the 'Crooked Tree,' Downes was able to visit this tree to document and photograph it. During the trip to visit the 'Crooked Tree' Downes stopped to visit a massive cottonwood tree near Kishwaukee Valley. Greg Prochnow originally located this cottonwood with a circumference of over 23 feet. The author has found many examples of cottonwoods, oaks, and other species that are native to the midwest that have grown to become enormous. Most of these species, if given the opportunity, will continue to grow to these massive proportions.

North of Peoria, along the Illinois River, there are many wildlife refuges and state parks. Downes was contacted by local resident and tour guide Dean Dunn about several Trail Marker Trees in some of the state parks. Downes met Mr. Dunn in Starved Rock State Park. In previous years the author had documented Trail Marker

This small sign has been put near the Trail Marker Tree that is located on the Girl Scout Camp. Photo taken by Greg Prochnow.

This Trail Marker Tree and the double trunk Trail Marker Tree seen on the next page, appear very close together. They are located in Starved Rock State Park. First photo taken by Greg Prochnow, second photo taken by Brian Buchholz

This photo taken by the author shows a view of Mattheissen State Park near the Trail Marker Tree located here.

Dennis next to the base of the ancient cottonwood tree, the diameter of this tree measures over seven feet. Photo taken by Greg Prochnow.

Trees in Starved Rock; the trees Mr. Dunn located were in fact trees that Downes had already documented. Years earlier, Lake County Forest Preserve employee, Brian Buchholz, had informed him about the trees. In Starved Rock there are three Trail Marker Trees located within a close vicinity to each other along the edge of a bluff. The author also has documentation that Frank R. Grover had visited, photographed, and documented Trail Marker Trees at Starved Rock; Grover wrote about these trees in his paper in 1905. Mr. Dunn and Downes went to the nearby Matthiessen State Park, where Mr. Dunn showed Downes a Double Trunk Trail Marker Tree that was located just off of a hiking trail. Then Mr. Dunn and the author traveled west to Chair Tree Park, near Lake Thunderbird and Putnam. Mr. Dunn had worked in the area as a young man and remembered the park that had been named after the Trail Marker Tree. This Trail Marker Tree, beloved by the locals and called the Chair Tree (also Senachwine Tree), was commemorated with a dedication ceremony in 1973. The Putnam County Historical Society along with the American Central Corporation helped to make the dedication possible. They also created a memorial sign, still standing, that reads:

The Senachwine Tree

This Indian Trail Marker is Dedicated to Potawatomi Chief Senachwine and to the Lake Thunderbird Property

Owners Present and Future Who Seek Out the Joys of Nature and Make Them Part of Their Lives.

Putnam County Historical Society
American Central Corporation
Lake Thunderbird
June 3, 1973

This Trail Marker Tree is said to be marking an Indian trail that led from Hennipen to Nauvoo and on to the Mississippi River. Chief Senachwine was of the River Potawatomi and known to be an apostle of peace in the area. His grave in the Illinois River Valley burial ground, half a mile north of Putnam, is said to be the highest mound and he was the last Indian to be buried there.

Southern Illinois

Southern Illinois is rich in Native American history and known for its beautiful and diverse landscape. Two of the wonders in the area include the Cahokia Mounds, made by ancient Mississippian mound builders, and the Garden of the Gods, created by nature. Southern Illinois is also located at the confluence of the Wabash, Missouri, Ohio, and Mississippi Rivers making this area accessible to travelers and an area of fertile river valleys. Some believe Southern Illinois received its name 'Little Egypt' because of the land's similarity to Egypt's Nile delta. The author was

The memorial sign near the Trail Marker Tree in Chair Tree Park.

Dean Dunn standing behind the massive Trail Marker Tree, called the Senachwine Tree and Chair Tree. Photo taken by the author.

The author examining the Double Trunk Trail Marker Tree in Mattheissen State Park. Photo taken by Dean Dunn.

Dennis next to an example of the rugged and dangerous terrain in the region of the Shawnee National Forest.

fortunate to live in the area of Southern Illinois for a number of years and was able to enjoy the beautiful outdoor wonders. The author frequently visited the Garden of the Gods and Giant City State Park.

Although it is known that there were numerous Trail Marker Trees in Southern Illinois, this area of the state does not have a great deal of documentation about these historical landmarks. In a 1940 *Wisconsin Archeologist* (Volume 21) article, *Trail Marking Trees*, Raymond Janssen is quoted saying that numerous Trail Marker Trees can be seen in Southern Illinois. Also, Robert Jackson, president of the Williamson County Historical Society, confirmed information the author had about Wayman Presley. Mr. Presley was a well-known tour guide and founder of Presley Tours, now a successful international business. During Mr. Presley's early tours (1950s) in Southern Illinois he would point out the existing Trail Marker Trees as part of his tours. Mr. Jackson was also able to attend a presentation about the Trail Marker Trees in the area by Mr. Presley. Southern Illinois resident, John O'Dell, author of *River to River Trail Guide* and outdoor enthusiast, affirmed the importance of the Trail Marker Trees in marking paths between the river systems. With Southern Illinois' location at the confluence of the four main rivers, safe portage would be a necessity of travel. Southern Illinois continues to reveal significant parts of its Native American history.

Dennis and a group of friends traveling from Makanda to Giant City and on to the Garden of the Gods in 1972.

In the late 1960's Downes hiking at Giant City State Park. Photo by Jim Siano.

A REMINDER OF OLD INDIAN D[

This photo appeared in the 1910 *Book of the North Shore* courtesy of the Chicago Historical Society. This Trail Marker Tree is said to be located in the Lakeside area.

This photograph appeared in the 1920 *Daily News*; it showed a Trail Marker Tree located in the Palos Township area.

The author examining the remains of a possible Trail Marker Tree that he was sent to by a local historian. Photo by Greg Prochnow.

following page
This ancient bur oak is estimated to be at least 500 years old and is the largest of its species in the state of Illinois, according to the DNR. This bur oak stands near Mount Pleasant on the Stoke Family property in Southern Illinois.

This map entitled "Indian Trails and Villages of Chicago and of Cook, DuPage, and Will Counties, Ills." was one of many maps created by Albert Scharf in the early 1900s. Courtesy of the Chicago History Museum.

Chicago

Today Chicago is the most populated city in the state of Illinois; it is a hub of commerce, industry, and infrastructure. Located along the southern end of Lake Michigan, in its early days Chicago became an important transportation hub between the eastern and western parts of the country. Due to its location and the Chicago Portage, this area was always a highly traveled location. Upon the arrival of the first Europeans, the Chicago area was inhabited by the Native Americans, including the Potawatomi (Neshnabek), Sauk, and Miami. The first documented non-native settler to Chicago was Jean Baptiste Pointe du Sable, now referred to as the founder of Chicago. Due to the rapid expansion and growth of the city, the Trail Marker Trees soon disappeared from the Chicago landscape. However, before the rapid growth of the city began, the Trail Marker Trees were said to be the most numerous in the region of Chicago, according to a 1940 article in *Wisconsin Archeologist*.

Although the city of Chicago does not have many documented examples of living Trail Marker Trees, it does have countless connections to the Trail Marker Tree Study. The Chicago Historical Society (now the Chicago History Museum), founded in 1856, still holds several early documented references to the Trail Marker Trees. In the proceedings of the Twenty First Congress of the National Society Daughters of the American Revolution (1912), a clear connection between Chicago and the Trail Marker Tree study is made; *"The history*

INDIAN TRAILS
AND
VILLAGES OF CHICAGO
AND OF
COOK, DUPAGE AND
WILL COUNTIES, ILLS.
(1804)
AS SHOWN BY
WEAPONS AND IMPLEMENTS
OF THE STONE-AGE.

COPYRIGHTED
1900 & 1901
ALBERT F. SCHARF.

~ INDEX ~
INDIAN VILLAGES, (NUMBERED.)
MINOR INDIAN VILLAGES _____
INDIAN CAMPS _____
CHIPPING STATIONS _____
PRINCIPLE INDIAN TRAILS
LETTERED AND NUMBERED ____
PORTAGE _____
SPRINGS _____
HEIGHTS AND
SIGNAL STATIONS _____
INDIAN MOUNDS _____
EFFIGY MOUND
LIZARD _____
MOUND BUILDERS
TRAIL _____

SCALE OF MAP
5/16 IN. TO MILE.

N
W — E

of the Indian Trail Trees of the North Shore of Chicago has
been known and handed down to the three generations
of early and present American white residents of Chicago and
suburbs, from the Indians themselves, who lived around here
until 1836 in large numbers, and when they immigrated west
of the Mississippi, a few stayed here for twenty years or more.
So the location and purpose of these Indian Trail Trees is as
much a part of our local history as Fort Dearborn or any
other landmark."

Three key Chicago historians were also documented by
the D.A.R. for their efforts in the Trail Marker Tree study.
Professor Fredrick Starr, head of the Department of
Anthropology at Chicago University, was considered to
have knowledge exceeding any other at the time about the
Native Americans and their customs. Professor Starr
contacted the D.A.R. to express his interest in the Trail
Marker Trees and encourage their efforts to preserve the trees.
The Trail Marker Trees were brought to his attention by
Charles S. Raddin. Mr. Raddin graduated from Northwestern
University with a Master of Science and became a director
and vice president of the Chicago Academy of Sciences and
vice president of the Evanston Historical Society. Mr. Raddin
wrote many articles that appeared in the *Chicago Evening*
Post about local history and science, including the Trail
Marker Trees. The president of the Evanston Historical Society,
Frank R. Grover, read his scholarly paper, *Some Indian*
Landmarks of the North Shore, to the Chicago Historical

Gary Johnson, President of the Chicago History Museum, at a meeting with the author.

The bronze plaque honoring the Old Treaty Elm.

Downes standing with Janet Davies at the Trail Marker Tree Exhibit held at 432 East Grand Avenue, Chicago.

The author at the Emergency Services Fundraiser, Grand Ballroom Navy Pier, where the Trail Marker Tree exhibit was displayed as part of the event. The Fundraiser was sponsored by the Catholic Charities.

Society in 1905. This paper explained and referenced numerous Trail Marker Trees in the area; the Society printed this paper and kept it in their collections.

The Chicago Historical Society provided a photo of a Trail Marker Tree from the Lakeside area for the *Book of the North Shore*, published in 1910. In 1911, the Daughters of the American Revolution displayed a commemorative bronze plaque honoring a Trail Marker Tree at the historic Blackstone Hotel. This plaque would later be installed next to a Trail Marker Tree in Glencoe. In response to the D.A.R.'s plaque, an area resident questioned the authenticity of the Trail Marker Trees. The D.A.R. was able to answer this area resident with the verification of several experts including Dr. Frank Grover, Jens Jensen (landscape architect, superintendent of Humboldt Park, and member of the Outer Park Belt Commission), and Jacob Prost (City Forester and superintendent of city parks). As part of the dedication ceremony for placing the bronze plaque, Jens Jensen also made an address "The Indian Trail Trees in Cook County and How They Were Bent." Albert F. Scharf, a valued historian and cartographer, kept a newspaper article, *Will Dedicate Indian Trail Tree Tablet*, about this event in his own personal collection. This collection is now on file at the Chicago History Museum.

In 1920, an article, *A Reminder of Old Indian Days*, (*The Daily News*) pictured a Trail Marker Tree from the Palos Township area. The article discussed Frank R. Grover's research that was kept by the Chicago Historical Society. According

to Grover's research there were 11 'Indian trees' in just this area near and around this township. Later in 1934, Dr. Raymond Janssen wrote an article, *Indian Trail Trees*, for the American Forestry Association in which he states, "About 75 of these old trail trees are still standing within the suburban area of Chicago..."

In the northern part of Chicago, near Forest Glen, a bronze plaque placed on a boulder still remains near the corner of Rodgers and Caldwell Avenues. This bronze plaque honors and marks the spot of the "Old Treaty Elm." The bronze plaque is inscribed: *"Old Treaty Elm. The tree which stood here until 1933, marked the Northern Boundary of the Fort Dearborn Reservation, the trail to Lake Geneva, the center of Billy Caldwell's (Chief Sauganash) Reservation, and the site of the Indian Treaty of 1835. Erected by Chicago's Charter Jubilee. Authenticated by Chicago Historical Society, 1937."* Billy Caldwell (Chief Sauganash) was known for serving as a mediator between the Native Americans and the American government. Caldwell also was instrumental in saving several lives during the Fort Dearborn Massacre, including those of the Kinzie family. The treaty signed in 1829 at Prairie Du Chien (Wisconsin) awarded Caldwell 1,600 acres in North Chicago, marked by the Indian Boundary Line. According to the Northwest Chicago Historical Society there was a bent tree, a Boundary Marker Tree that marked this territory.

In the 1960's, May Theilgaard Watts, a Chicago resident well known for being a naturalist and conservationist, wrote

The author stands in front of his Trail Marker Tree sculpture during the Trolley Tour celebration.

Dan Melone standing in front of a Trail Marker Tree he located in the Palos area. Photo taken by archeologist Dan Melone.

The grafted 'double tree' is shown here drawn by Albert F. Scharf after seeing the tree in 1869. Photo courtesy of the Chicago History Museum.

a column for the *Chicago Tribune* entitled *Nature Afoot*. Watts graduated from the University of Chicago after studying botany and ecology. She also went on to work at the Morton Arboretum for many years. In her early years she would collaborate with Jens Jensen to save the wild prairie near Ravinia, even publishing a booklet, *Ravinia: her Charms and Destiny* (1936). One of Watts' later columns from *Nature Afoot* was dedicated to the Trail Marker Trees and to their unfortunate disappearance from the landscape.

In the 1990s the author was able to attend a lecture by Helen Hornbeck Tanner at the Newberry Library. The Newberry Library is a nationally renowned research library founded in the 1800s. Helen Hornbeck Tanner is the nation's foremost researcher and disseminator of Native American history of the Great Lakes Region. Years after attending Tanner's lecture, Downes was able to conduct a phone interview with Tanner and discuss the progression of the study about the Trail Marker Trees. During this interview Tanner confirmed her knowledge of the Trail Marker Trees throughout the Great Lakes Region; Tanner also discussed the use of grafted trees with the author. Grafted trees were used to convey information near navigable rivers and waterways. Albert F. Scharf documented a grafted tree located along the Chicago River, not far from the intersection of Clybourn and Fullerton Avenues. Scharf was shown this tree by local hunters in 1869; this tree was grafted from a red oak tree and a pignut hickory tree and formed a perfect 'H'.

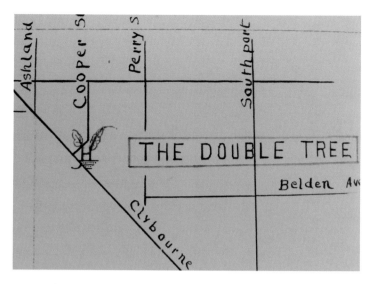

Today there are few remaining Trail Marker Trees in and around Chicago. One Trail Marker Tree that is still standing can be found on the grounds of the Ridgemoor Country Club, as was discussed earlier in the chapter. Two other Trail Marker Trees in the Chicago area were brought to the author's attention by archeologist, Dan Melone. Melone sent Downes photographs of trees he had come across and believed to be Trail Marker Trees. One tree is located in Jurgensen Woods, a known archeological site. The author was able to match up this Trail Marker Tree with a photo from a 1940 article, *Trail Signs of the Indians*, in Natural History by Raymond Janssen. Here the same tree was pictured 70 years earlier and it has changed little since. The other tree is located in the Palos area. Dan Melone has worked for the Field Museum and is currently working with the Raupp Museum in Buffalo Grove, Illinois.

The author continues to have many ties to the Chicago area with his ongoing study. Downes has had several Trail Marker Tree exhibits at many locations including Navy Pier and Soldier Field during special events. After viewing one of the author's exhibits held at 432 East Grand Avenue, Janet Davies, entertainment reporter and host and executive producer of *190 North*, stated: *"After having seen Dennis Downes' beautifully revealing exhibit of Indian Trail Markers plus his expert and haunting related art-work, I am truly impressed that one man has taken it upon himself to educate and enlighten us on the splendor and importance of these rapidly disappearing symbols of Native America. Downes has obviously spent untold hours making this part of his life's work."* Downes also had a bronze Trail Marker Tree sculpture displayed downtown near Gill Park for a year as part of the Lakefront Sculpture Exhibition. Through the years the author has been able to utilize the many historical resources the city of Chicago has to offer, including the Newberry Library, the Chicago History Museum, and archives of the local chapters of the D.A.R. (Fort Dearborn Chapter). Recently, Gary Johnson, president of the Chicago History Museum, has become involved in the Trail Marker Tree study. The author presented his study to Johnson at the museum. Afterwards, Johnson was able to view the bronze Trail Marker Tree sculpture while it was on display downtown. Johnson said, "The bronze Trail Marker by Dennis Downes is a powerful reminder of a byegone era. As Chicago celebrates its 175th anniversary as a city in 2012, it is too easy to forget that for centuries and centuries before then, this very same land was home to countless generations of inhabitants. They left their marks in the trees, some of which still survive to point out the paths that those people followed. Now, an important local artist has left a permanent representation of those trees. This artistic creation will help us to remember the people who were here first and the paths that they blazed." Without the Chicago History Museum (Chicago Historical Society), much of the documentation on the Trail Marker Tree study may not be available today. Their exceptional collection has been an important resource for the author. Chicago has been an

The author's Life-Size Realistic Trail Marker Tree sculpture and informational plaque have been on exhibit at the Lake County Discovery Museum in Wauconda, Illinois for the last six years. It has been the focus of numerous lectures and educational visits helping to teach thousands of children and adults about the historical significance of the Native American Trail Marker Trees throughout our country.

integral part of the past and ongoing Trail Marker Tree study.

The state of Illinois seems to be the major source of written documentation about these culturally altered landmarks. For nearly 200 years, these trees have been referred to as Indian Trail Trees and Marker Trees. Without some of the aforementioned researchers, the knowledge of the Trail Marker Trees may have been lost to history. Instead, thanks to their efforts, there has been a continuous flow of documentation throughout the history of the state. Many other states have started their research about Trail Marker Trees from information they gathered in Illinois. In some cases individuals learned about the Trail Marker Trees in Illinois and would move to other states, such as Laura Hubler. Laura Hubler learned about the trees in Chicago after seeing her first Trail Marker Tree in Kenilworth, Illinois. Hubler later went on to record similar trees she saw while living in Missouri and the surrounding area and began referring to these trees as Thong Trees. Hubler used this name because of a method some believe was used to shape the trees. Elaine Jordan also lived and worked in Illinois in her early years and later, in Georgia, used many names to refer to the Trail Marker Trees and other deformed trees including thong trees, message trees, horse and rider trees, and treasure trees. Both Hubler and Jordan helped to spread the knowledge and awareness of the Trail Marker Trees and located several living examples. However, by using alternate names and including examples of younger trees that were simply deformed, they

may have also created some confusion. The author has chosen to use the original terminology for these trees, found in some of the earliest documentation. This decision was based on other early research in anthropology texts. In the *Nomenclature of Anthropology* (1892) by Daniel Brinton, M.D., LL.D., an accepted rule for anthropology is stated; "No new term should be coined when there already exists one in the literature of the science which conveys the meaning." Maintaining the same terminology for the Trail Marker Trees will make it easier for future researchers to study and preserve these trees.

Chapter Four

WISCONSIN

The state of Wisconsin is a Great Lakes state, bordered by Lake Michigan to the east and partly by Lake Superior to the north. Wisconsin is known for its beautiful and varied scenery. The state offers dense forests, rich farmland, high bluffs, sandstone formations, rolling hills, waterfalls, glacial lakes, and many rivers. The state's name originated from the Native American language and although there are many different variations and theories, they all revolve around the Wisconsin River and its red coloration due to the sandstone lining on its banks. Throughout the state's history there have been many different groups of Native inhabitants that have been traced back to the Ice Ages.

Between 1000 B.C. and 1000 A.D. Wisconsin became the heart of the Effigy Mound Culture; many of the animal shaped mounds can still be seen across the landscape. Starting in 1000 A.D. the Aztalan culture began to thrive. The Aztalan seemed to have many cultural traditions in common with the nearby Cahokia, in Illinois. Today, the remains of the Aztalan are considered to be the state's "crown jewel" of their archeological sites by the Wisconsin Department of Natural Resources. When the first Europeans arrived in Wisconsin, many Native American tribes were living in the area including the Winnebago, Potawatomi, Sauk, Menominee, Fox, Kickapoo, and Ojibwa. The first European to come to the area was Jean Nicolet, most likely near present-day Green Bay. Wisconsin officially became a state in 1848 and since then has become an outdoor haven for tourists from across the country. Known for its many state and national parks, resorts, and attractions, Wisconsin remains a popular tourist destination.

Milwaukee
The author has many ties to the state of Wisconsin starting when he was just a child during camping trips to Shawano, one of his family's favorite spots. More recently, while researching the Trail Marker Trees, he has made numerous trips to all areas of the state and worked with various organizations including the DNR, historical societies, and even the Milwaukee Public Museum. After over a decade of research focused on the Native American Trail Marker Trees, Downes was referred

page 137
The beautiful Lake Geneva, the historic Louise built in 1902 is still part of the Geneva Lake Cruise Line today.

This double trunk Trail Marker Tree stood in Twin Lakes guiding the Native Americans along the land bridge between Lake Elizabeth and Lake Mary. Photo courtesy of the Lake County Museum Archives.

The author was given this photo in the late 1980's from an Antioch resident of this triple trunk Trail Marker Tree that stood in the Twin Lakes area and was said to mark an Indian village. Unfortunately, this tree has long since fallen.

This map from 1887 shows the path the Native Americans would have taken upon following the double trunk Trail Marker Tree.

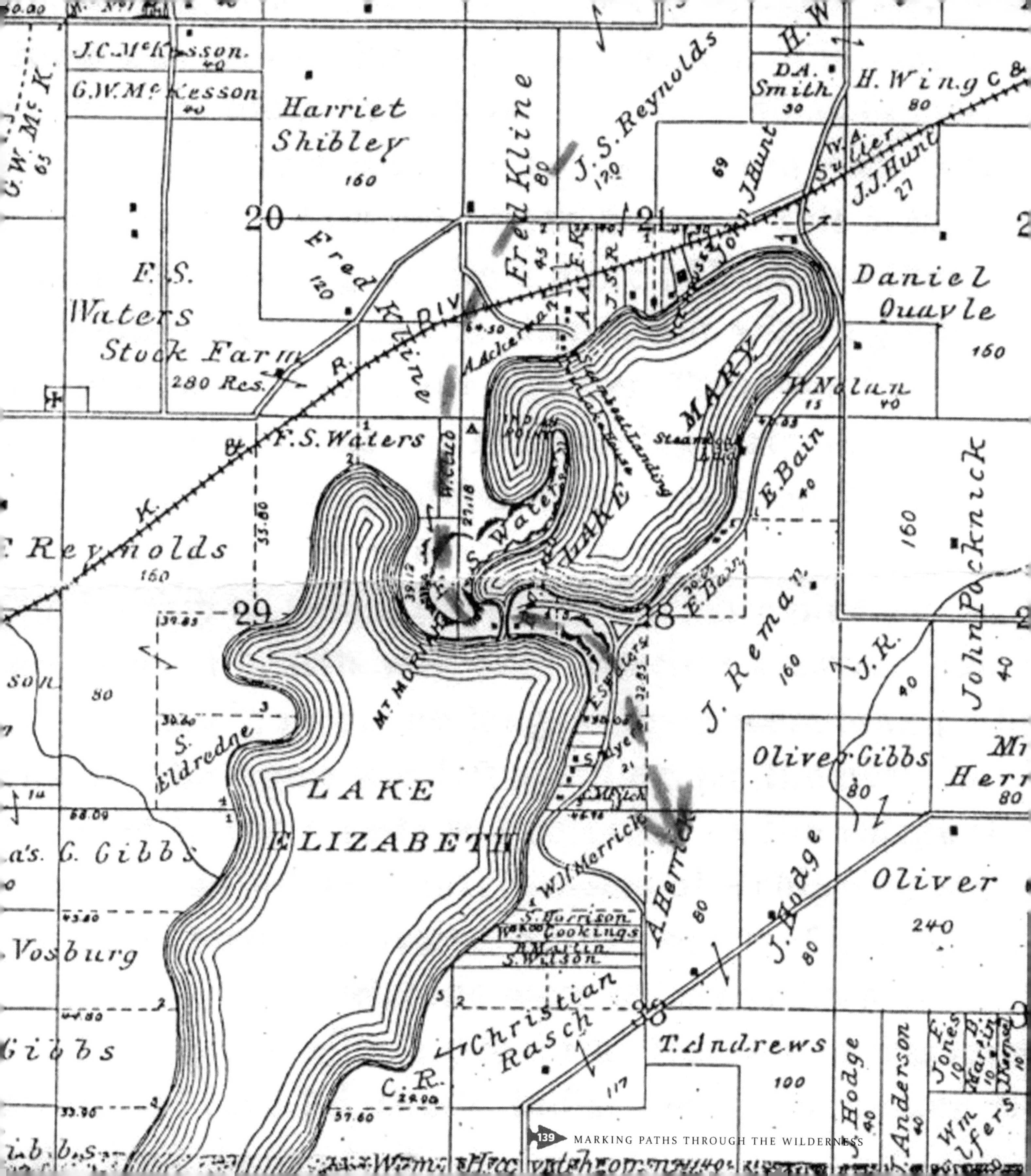

J.C. McKesson.

G.W. McKesson

Harriet
Shibley
160

Fred Kline
80

J.S. Reynolds
120

J. Hunt

D.A.
Smith
30

H. Wing
80

C. &

J.J. Hunt
27

20

21

F.S.
Waters
Stock Farm
280 Res.

Fred Kline
120

Fred Kline

W.A. Sutter

Daniel
Quayle

160

F.S. Waters

S. Waters

LAKE MARY

H. Nolan
15

E. Bain
40

160

T. Reynolds
160

LAKE

Steamboat

E. Bain

29

28

E. Bain

S. Eldredge
80

J. Reman
160

J.R.
40

John Packnick
40

LAKE
ELIZABETH

Mt. Mor

Oliver Gibbs
80

Herr
80

a's. G. Gibbs

W. Herrick

A. Herrick
60

J. Hodge
80

Oliver
240

Vosburg

S. Harrison
Cookings
A. Martin
S. Wilson

Gibbs

C.R.

Christian
Rasch
117

T. Andrews
100

J. Hodge
40

Anderson

Jones

Martin

to Ann McMullen, Ph.D. of the Milwaukee Public Museum in 1995. McMullen was the curator of North American Ethnology and the section head of the Anthropology Department. McMullen helped make several connections for Downes including drawing his attention to *Wisconsin Archeologist*, the longest continuously published archeological journal in North America. This journal contained many references to the Trail Marker Trees dating to the early 1900's. McMullen also recommended various other periodicals and suggested areas where Trail Marker Trees could be located that were helpful to the author's study. After working with Downes, McMullen stated, "*His research into this area and knowledge of it is unique. I know of no other person who has so systematically searched out references to these trees and spent long days and weeks locating surviving examples.*" McMullen and the Milwaukee Public Museum served as a valuable resource to the author's continuing study.

According to the *Milwaukee Journal*, 1925, the city of Milwaukee was actually built upon over 200 Indian Mounds. A special Marker Tree was said to be located near the intersection of Wells and Thirteenth Streets through the mid 1800s. This large beech tree had a notable carving of an Indian figure that pointed the way to two trails; one trail would lead to Chicago and the other trail would lead to Green Bay. This tree was also referred to in the *Wisconsin Archeologist* volumes 19 and 46.

Twin Lakes

The village of Twin Lakes is located along the Illinois border in western Kenosha County. Twin Lakes has two documented Trail Marker Trees. The first, a double trunk Trail Marker Tree, was located overlooking the northeast bay of Lake Elizabeth. This tree guided to the trail that crossed the land bridge separating the two lakes. This Trail Marker Tree would allow the Native Americans to get from one side of the lakes to the other in a significantly shorter amount of time. This double trunk Trail Marker Tree was documented by Phil Sanders, a noted conservationist, author, and historian. Sanders wrote an article about this Trail Marker Tree that was included in Volume 46 of *Wisconsin Archeologist*. The other known Twin Lakes tree was a triple trunk Trail Marker Tree.

Bristol

The village of Bristol is located in southeastern Wisconsin, near the Illinois border. Bristol is known as the green and natural corner of Kenosha County and it strives to keep the natural feel of the town. A friend of the author, Ron Bernardi, told Dennis about a locally well-known Indian Marker Tree that stood in the village of Bristol. This tree has been called the "Pointer Tree" by the locals and is a non-traditional Marker Tree; it still stands today in the Pringle Nature Center. The Pringle Family has lived in Kenosha County for over a century and they have always taken an interest in nature and their environment. The Pringle Family donated funds to help

The Native American Pointer Tree located at the Pringle Nature Center in Bristol, Wisconsin.

This photograph taken by the author shows the Sacred Medicine Wheel located in Lake Geneva, Wisconsin. Knonozo (Steve Young) , Potawatomi historical expert, brought Downes to this rare site that he discovered. This Sacred Medicine Wheel is considered to be a unique example by the Lake Geneva Potawatomi Committee; this Wheel is made of 18 boulders not the traditional 16 boulders. The two additional 'marker stones' pointed in the direction of the nearby Conical Mound.

Perry Crakes and his son, Dale, an accomplished Eagle Scout.

establish this nature center. Robert Pringle confirmed the history of the Pointer Tree and told the naturalist at Pringle Nature Center that his family has known the tree's Native American ties for generations.

Although there is no written or photographic documentation about any other Trail Marker Trees in the Bristol area, Knonozo, Potawatomi historical expert, told the author about three Trail Marker Trees that once stood in this village. These three trees were traditional Trail Marker Trees. One of the trees pointed westerly to a trail leading to Mukwonago and the other two trees pointed northerly to trails leading to Milwaukee and Green Bay.

Paris

The rural farm town of Paris is located just north of Bristol. This town has kept developers out to maintain its open lands and farm community feel. The Saint John the Baptist Catholic Church was founded in Paris in 1859 and is still there today. Longtime friend of the author, Perry Crakes, informed the author about a Trail Marker Tree he came across in the town of Paris. Perry is an adult leader with the Boy Scouts of America; he and his son Dale have been involved with the Boy Scouts for years. Crakes has been able to educate some of the local Boy Scout troops about the Trail Marker Trees with information he had received from Downes. The author was able to join Crakes to visit the Trail Marker Tree in Paris, located on private property. This massive tree is over three feet in

diameter; the bend in this Trail Marker Tree has begun to fall and change shape under the immense weight of the tree. Years later, the author was informed that this same tree had been damaged after being struck by lightning during a storm. Greg Prochnow joined Dennis to document the tree after it had sustained the significant damage.

Kettle Moraine State Forest, Lapham Peak

This beautiful area was formed over 10,000 years ago during the Ice Age when a glacier covered much of the area. Lapham Peak is the highest point in Waukesha County and provides a stunning view of the surrounding lands. There were four Trail Marker Trees standing in the Lapham Peak area of the Kettle Moraine State Forest. In 1951, Mr. Charles P. Fox wrote an article *Indian Highway Signs* that was published by the Milwaukee Public Museum in their *LORE Magazine*. In this article, Fox identified two Trail Marker Trees in the Lapham Peak area that were located close together. Later in 1965, Dr. Robert Ritzenthaler discussed these fine examples of Trail Marker Trees in his article *Trail Marker Trees*, published in the *Wisconsin Archeologist*. Dr. Ritzenthaler was the editor of this journal for more than 20 years; he also served as the president of the Wisconsin Archeological Society in 1951, and worked for years as the curator of anthropology at the Milwaukee Public Museum until 1972. To honor the devotion of Dr. Ritzenthaler, the officers of the Wisconsin Archeological Society created the Robert E. Ritzenthaler Service Award.

Downes examining the Paris Trail Marker Tree in winter when there was less brush and undergrowth around the tree.

This old plaque stands nearby the two Trail Marker Trees in Kettle Moraine State Forest.

Downes and Brian Buchholz standing by the two distinct Trail Marker Trees decades after the photo taken by Dr. Ritzenthaler. During the many years between photographs, numerous young trees have grown up around these two old Trail Marker Trees.

On a later visit to the area, Dennis located the marsh referred to in the informational plaque. Today the marsh has an elaborate walking path built across it. Photo taken by the author.

pages 144–145
This photograph of the two Trail Marker Trees located near Lapham Peak was part of Dr. Ritzenthaler's collection and appeared in the Wisconsin Archeologist. Courtesy of the Milwaukee Public Museum.

The author standing with Brian and Nadean Buchholz near one of the other two Trail Marker Trees located in the Kettle Moraine State Park. The two great arms coming from the tree have since been removed.

Downes examining the fourth Trail Marker Tree located in the Kettle Moraine State Forest.

Downes standing near the bronze plaque marking the Half-Way Tree in Brodhead. The giant bur oak marks the halfway point between Lake Michigan and the Mississippi River; it was accurately paced off by Indian runners.

The bronze plaque placed by the Brodhead Historical Society marking the Half-Way Tree.

The author had the article written by Dr. Ritzenthaler in his files, but had not personally documented these Trail Marker Trees until he was contacted by Amy Lou Jenkins. Jenkins contacted Downes about these same two trees located in the Lapham Peak area after visiting his educational website about the Trail Marker Trees. Jenkins met with Downes and gave him directions to the trees. He was able to locate these two Trail Marker Trees with arborist Brian Buchholz and horticulturist Nadean Buchholz. Near the Trail Marker Trees an old informational plaque was installed that reads: "*Indian Marker Trees; Before white settlers arrived in Wisconsin, Prairie Pottowatami Indians lived in this area, establishing a village along Lake Nagawicka and hunting and gathering the abundant wildlife. To find their way to and from the village and sources of food and water, these people bent small sapling trees over and secured them to the ground. As the trees matured, they grew into pointers, precursors to today's road signs. These two trees and others like them point west toward a marsh.*" Jenkins would contact Downes again to further her understanding and would later mention him and these trees in her book..., *Every Natural Fact: Five Seasons of Open Air Parenting.* This pattern of two Trail Marker Trees standing side by side occurs throughout the country, and historians have said this practice was to convey additional information about the area.

After the author's initial visit to the Kettle Moraine State Forest, he returned several times over the next

This photograph, taken in 1922, shows a young woman sitting on a Trail Marker Tree that marked the same trail as the Half-Way Tree. This Trail Marker Tree is also located in the area of Brodhead. Photograph courtesy Betty Earleywine, The Brodhead Historical Society.

Nearly 100 years after the earlier photograph, the author stands near the Brodhead Trail Marker Tree.

This photograph taken over sixty years ago shows two park visitors standing in the Blue Mound Trail Marker Tree.

Doug Meier and the author next to the double trunk Trail Marker Tree in Black Earth.

Dennis, his wife Gail, Brian and Nadean Buchholz standing behind the Blue Mound Trail Marker Tree that has begun to show its age.

few years. The author was able to locate two additional Trail Marker Trees in the area that the earlier mentioned plaque may have been alluding to.

The Halfway Tree, Brodhead

The city of Brodhead is located centrally in the southern part of Wisconsin. This area welcomes outdoor enthusiasts to enjoy their beautiful bluffs, the Sugar River, and many wild flowers. This historic town, founded in 1856, has kept its history alive with the help of local historians and the Brodhead Historical Society. Brodhead is known for its famous Half-Way Tree, just south of the city. The Brodhead Historical Society had a bronze plaque placed to commemorate this tree's significance; the plaque is inscribed: "The Half-Way Tree; This bur oak marks the halfway point between Lake Michigan and the Mississippi River. Paced off by Indian runners and confirmed by U.S. survey in 1832. Spring Grove Township, Green County-Wisconsin. Courtesy of the Brodhead Historical Society." This route from Lake Michigan to the Mississippi was the shortest distance and part of this route later became a stage coach route. The stage coach route eventually became Highway 81. As late as 1861 there are records of an Indian chief camping near the Half-Way Tree and telling the Warner Family (who owned the property at the time) about the importance of the tree. Betty Earleywine of the Brodhead Historical Society gave the author information about another Trail Marker Tree located on this route. Dennis was able to locate this tree during one of his visits to the area. This Trail Marker Tree was photographed in 1922 and is still standing today; this tree would have been one of many Trail Marker Trees along the course of this trail connecting the two bodies of water.

Lake Mills, Rock Lake

The city of Lake Mills is located north of Brodhead. The area of Lake Mills is surrounded by natural beauty from the crystal clear waters of Rock Lake and its mysterious pyramidal mounds, to its location along the Glacial Drumlin Trail, and the nearby Aztalan State Park. The Aztalan State Park is an important archeological site. Today there are still many mounds remaining in the area that have been examined by leading archeologists. Some of these mounds had a large post placed in the center surrounded by clay and gravel. These large posts rose up from the center of the mounds and would have been visible for miles. Just as the Effigy Mound culture would have used their many shaped mounds as references when navigating throughout their region, archeologists believe these mounds and posts were 'marker mounds' and would have marked the site for travelers. Along with the 'marker mounds' in the area, there is also documentation of a Trail Marker Tree that stood in the city of Lake Mills. This traditional Trail Marker Tree was photographed in 1967 by a postmaster, Kenneth Kisow. Mr. Kisow sent the photograph to the Wisconsin Archeological Society after reading an article in *Wisconsin Archeologist* about the Trail Marker Trees.

The author and Brian Buchholz looking down onto the valley from the top of Blue Mound, the highest point.

This photograph of the massive basswood Trail Marker Tree in Brothertown appeared in the Sheboygan Press in 1968.

The author sitting in this odd Marker Tree that is also located in the Blue Mound State Park.

This traditional Trail Marker Tree in La Farge can be seen upon the ridge from a great distance. Photograph taken by Jim Jordan.

This Trail Marker Tree stood near the shores of Green Lake and was documented by Edward McCabe of Milwaukee, this photograph appeared in the Wisconsin Archeologist.

Madison, Black Earth, and Blue Mounds.

The book, *Historic American Trees*, written in 1922, has a drawing of the Madison 'Indian Trail Tree' gracing its cover. This Marker Tree had one branch conspicuously bent to indicate the direction of the trail. Another Marker Tree located in Madison, near what today is the intersection of Elm and Van Hise Streets, was documented having four branches pointing in four separate directions. This Marker Tree was located at the intersection of two Indian trails.

Just west of Madison in the town of Black Earth is documentation of a large effigy mound and two Trail Marker Trees. This rare effigy mound was referred to as the "Man Mound" as it was shaped like a man. The body of the "Man Mound" pointed east and west, whereas, the arms of the mound pointed north and south, making this effigy mound directionally significant. This large effigy mound was over 700 feet in length; the head alone was 25 feet in diameter. Unfortunately, this "Man Mound" was leveled by building.

The author was contacted by Douglas Meier of the Wisconsin DNR Radio Communications, in regards to two Trail Marker Trees. Meier found both of these Trail Marker Trees and was able to locate a nearby fresh water spring that he believes these trees lead to. Dennis and two of his nephews, Sander and Axel, were able to meet Meier to see and document these Trail Marker Trees. Unfortunately, one of the trees fell before the author was able to see it. The remains of this Trail Marker Tree were still on the ground when Downes visited.

The author examining the La Farge Trail Marker Tree. Photo taken by Brian Buchholz.

Jim Jordan walking alongside the natural year-round spring.

Dennis shown by the large Trail Marker Tree in West Salem. Dennis was taken to the site by Jim Jordan

The permanent sign that stands next to the Trail Marker Tree in West Salem.

"Trail Tree Drive" named after the Trail Marker Tree standing alongside the road.

Further west is the village of Blue Mounds and the Blue Mound State Park, which is the highest point in southern Wisconsin. This state park has two documented Trail Marker Trees, one of which is still standing. Next to the remaining Trail Marker Tree is an informational sign that explains the significance of the Trail Marker Trees and states that the two Trail Marker Trees in the park lead to a clear flowing spring. The author was able to follow the direction of the remaining Trail Marker Tree and located the fresh water spring. One of the hiking trails in Blue Mound State Park is named "Indian Marker Tree Trail" after the oak Trail Marker Tree that was shaped by the Native Americans long ago. Also located on the grounds of the Blue Mound State Park is a unique Marker Tree. The author plans to investigate this white oak tree further and revisit it in the future.

Wisconsin Dells, Brothertown, Green Lake

The area of Wisconsin Dells is best known today for being the "Waterpark Capital of the world." However, Wisconsin Dells is also known for its beautiful and scenic glacially formed gorges and sandstone formations along the Wisconsin River. There have been two documented Trail Marker Trees in the Wisconsin Dells area. However, it is likely that there were many more that fell or were taken down before they could be documented. In 1941, Dr. Raymond Janssen wrote about the two Trail Marker Trees that were still standing in the area at the time. One of the two trees was located near the famous Stand

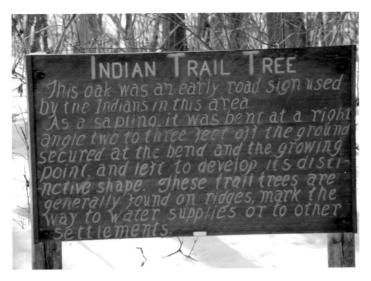

Rock. Raymond Gloede was involved in a dedication ceremony for an Illinois Trail Marker Tree in 1928, along with the Daughters of the American Revolution. Native Americans from the Wisconsin Dells area came down to participate in the ceremony. Later, Gloede was able to travel to the Wisconsin Dells to photograph living Trail Marker Trees and interview one of the chiefs that he had met at the ceremony in 1928.

Just northeast of the Wisconsin Dells in the town of Brothertown, a large basswood Trail Marker Tree was recorded. This town was named after the Brothertown Indians that moved to the area from New York. This Trail Marker Tree was photographed for an article in the *Sheboygan Press* in 1968 and appeared massive at the time.

The area around Green Lake, just west of Brothertown, has been documented to have a number of Trail Marker Trees. Charles E. Brown noted several Trail Marker Trees on the grounds of the Lawsonia, a golf course on the north side of Green Lake. Mr. Brown served as the curator for the State Historical Society of Wisconsin and the secretary of the Wisconsin Archeological Society. One traditional Trail Marker Tree stood near Oakwood Beach on the southeast shore of Green Lake. There were three Trail Marker Trees located on Camp Grow, a Boy Scout camp ground also near the southeast side of the lake. Dr. Robert Ritzenthaler photographed the Trail Marker Trees at Camp Grow.

La Crosse and Necedah Area

Necedah is located north of the Wisconsin Dells along the Yellow River and the Wisconsin River. Necedah is known for its conservation lands including the Necedah National Forest and the Necedah Wildlife Refuge. La Crosse is located along the Mississippi River and appeared attractive to its first non-native settlers because of its high bluffs along the River. Today La Crosse is known for being a university city, with three colleges and universities within the city, and for its many outdoor recreational activities ranging from water sports to cross country skiing.

Just south of La Crosse is the village of La Farge, located along the Kickapoo River. Along a ridge outside of the village there is a traditional Trail Marker Tree. This Trail Marker Tree can be seen from quite a distance because of the unique Trail Marker Tree shape. This tree points towards a nearby year-round fresh water spring. Local Trail Tree enthusiast, Jim Jordan located this tree and brought the author to see it. Jim has been working with Downes to locate trees in Wisconsin for many years. During the trip to see this traditional Trail Marker Tree, the author was able to meet the land owners and find out more about the surrounding land. The spring that the tree points to supplies fresh water year-round to the local wild-life, even during the winter the spring is running. North of La Farge in Necedah, a maple double trunk Trail Marker Tree located along the Yellow River. This tree was found by Kevin Murphy, a friend of Jim Jordan.

Downes and arborist Brian Buchholz met Jim Jordan on another trip in the village of West Salem; West Salem is located just north of La Crosse and west of Necedah. The old Trail Marker Tree located here has been a prominent part of the community for generations. This tree is commemorated with a permanent sign explaining the tree's significance and connection to the Native Americans. The street along which the tree is located is fittingly named Trail Tree Drive.

Oconto, Shawano, Park Falls

The city of Oconto, located along the shores of Green Bay, is known for its history of the Copper Culture. The Copper Culture State Park is home to the Old Copper Culture Cemetery, which is believed to be one of the oldest burial grounds in the nation; it is the oldest cemetery in Wisconsin, dating back to around 5000 B.C. When this burial ground was excavated a wide variety of copper tools and implements were found with the human remains. Many examples of these advanced copper tools and implements are on display within the Copper Culture State Park and Museum. Jim Jordan and his wife visited the Copper Culture State Park and Museum and viewed an old photograph of a Trail Marker Tree from the area that was on display; Jordan contacted the author and informed him about this photograph. Downes made an appointment with historian and author, Monette Bebow-Reinhard, the museum's curator, and Reinhard was able to give Downes some information

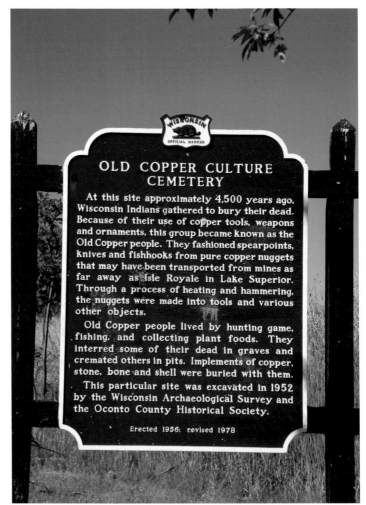

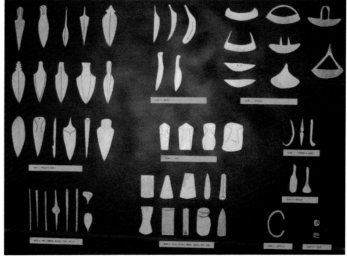

This sign denotes the area of the Old Copper Culture Cemetery in the Copper Culture State Park.

This Shawano souvenir flag has been in the author's family for generations. The photo shown in the opening of the flag is a photo of John and Matt Downes, the author's uncle and father in the 1920's.

An educational exhibit inside the Copper Culture State Park Museum showing examples of copper spear heads, hooks, and cutting tools.

about the Trail Marker Tree and an approximate location. Even with this information, the author was unable to locate the tree. Reinhard suggested Downes contact Donald Nerenhausen, a surveyor and past mayor of the city. With Nerenhausen's help, Downes was finally able to locate this Trail Marker Tree; the tree was standing behind a building that had been built after the original photograph seen in the museum was taken. The building prevented the Trail Marker Tree from being seen from the road. The author was able to talk with the home and property owner about the Trail Marker Tree and the surrounding property. The property owner was aware of an artesian well located on the property, not far from the tree. He also mentioned that Highway 51, running in front of the property, was originally a known Indian Trail. This tree is included in the Oconto County Historic and Archeological Sites, listed by the Oconto County Historical Society.

Shawano

The author's family has been visiting Shawano for camping trips for three generations. The town of Shawano has a warm northern woods feel and offers camping, hunting, fishing, water skiing. It is just a short trip to visit Lambeau Field. The area around Shawano is known for its American Indian history and modern ties with the Native Americans today. The Menominee Tribe were some of the early inhabitants of the Shawano area and can still be found there today. The town of Shawano is documented to have a Trail

☼	SACRED SPRING	⁙	STONE HEAPS
♡	BOULDER MORTAR	◬F	QUARRY, FLINT
⊘	GRINDSTONE BOULDER	◬	QUARRY, QUARTZITE
☘	SPIRIT STONE	◬	QUARRY, QUARTZ
↝	IMPLEMENT CACHE	◭	QUARRY, PIPESTONE
○	LODGE CIRCLE	◬C	QUARRY, CHLORITE
◌	STONE CIRCLE	◬S	QUARRY, STEATITE
☘	TRAIL TREE	▽C	QUARRY, COPPER
⊔	GRAVE	▽L	QUARRY, LEAD
⌷S	STONE GRAVE	⌒	CAVE HABITATION
⊔⊔	CEMETERY, MODERN	⌐	ROCK SHELTER
⊔⊔	CEMETERY, PREHISTORIC	🚶	PETROGLYPH

These are examples of archeological map symbols that were used on the atlas by Charles E. Brown. The symbol for the 'Trail Tree' can be seen in the left column.

Another nearby traditional Trail Marker Tree located by Downes in Park Falls. Photo taken by the author.

Dennis and Black Dog Miller standing by the double trunk Trail Marker Tree located near the Flambeau River.

Dennis and Black Dog Miller examining the Trail Marker Tree first located by Jim Jordan's sister in Park Falls.

This photograph is on display at the Copper Culture State Park Museum. The caption under the photograph reads: "An Oak 'trail marker tree' of undetermined age still points the way across Green Bay from what is now Oak Orchard. The tree is near an Indian Village site along an ancient trail which followed the West Green Bay shoreline." This photograph was taken before the home was built in front of the Trail Marker Tree.

Dennis and Greg Prochnow by the Oconto Trail Marker Tree decades after the previous photo was taken.

Marker Tree in a very early reference by Charles E. Brown. *Charles E. Brown Atlas*, 1924, was completed using Brown's manuscripts and record of antiquities. Brown was a respected historian and curator; he completed survey plats of early Wisconsin including symbols to indicate items of importance such as archeological sites and trails. On the atlas of Shawano a Trail Marker Tree is included. Mr. Brown's plats had a specific map symbol to depict 'Trail Trees.' The author and his wife, Gail, were able to locate this symbol on the Shawano atlas after hours of searching through scores of plats; the plats are very large and very detailed making it difficult to locate certain symbols.

Park Falls

The city of Park Falls is located northwest of the Shawano area and is along the banks of the Flambeau River. This city is considered a recreation paradise, offering almost every outdoor recreation activity along with calm and beautiful scenic surroundings. Near the town of Park Falls off of Highway 70, Jim Jordan's sister spotted a possible Trail Marker Tree while traveling. The author was able to contact friends, Black Dog and Ann Miller, who live in the area, and asked them to look into this tree further. Black Dog and Ann where able to locate the tree and send Dennis some photographs. Shortly thereafter, Dennis was able to make a trip to meet Black Dog and Ann to see the tree. Dennis and the Miller's researched the Trail Marker Tree and the surrounding area for several days. During this research the author was able to find two

other Trail Marker Trees in the area. He was also able to locate a shallow point in the nearby Flambeau River that would have provided safe crossing for the American Indians. It appeared that this path of safe crossing was what at least one of the Trail Marker Trees would have been guiding to in the past. The author plans to do further research in this area and to verify the age of these three Trail Marker Trees.

The Green Bay Trail Marker Tree Shaping Project

Currently in Green Bay, Jim O'Rourke and other history buffs are working towards the Road to Green Bay. This project hopes to establish a trail between Prairie Du Chien and Green Bay that will run along the proposed Heritage State Parkway. O'Rourke contacted the author about placing Trail Marker Trees along this trail to add further historical significance to the project.

The state of Wisconsin does not have nearly as many documented Trail Marker Trees as their neighboring state, Illinois. The clearest explanation for this is the Wisconsin lumber boom in the 1800s. The lumber industry began in Wisconsin in the early 1830s and was in full swing by 1840. The forests near rivers were the first to be hit hard. Later the railroad allowed loggers to go deeper into the woods. Lumbering became the backbone of Wisconsin's early economy. By the 1900s some forests in Wisconsin were totally cleared, eliminating almost all of the old growth forests throughout the state. Some loggers would have known the significance of the Trail Marker Trees and would have saved

Downes joined by Mayor James Schmitt, Beautification Committee Chairman Paul Hartman, and children from one of the participating schools planting one of the young oak trees that will later be shaped. Jim O'Rourke chose this location for the Trail Marker Tree along a locally significant waterway. Photo by Gail Spreen.

The award winning Trail Marker Tree float, created by the ARTgarage group, which was presented in the Green Bay Arbor Day Parade. Photo by Gail Spreen.

In Green Bay, Jim O'Rourke and Downes joined by one of the participating school groups during the tree planting ceremony as part of the event: *A New Twist in Time: Connecting the Past with the Future.*

The Flambeau River, the shallow area safe for fording can be seen in this photograph. Photo taken by the author.

them from the saw; however, many loggers were not aware of the historical significance of these trees. Since the lumber boom the state has replanted and conserved many forests across the state and Wisconsin is again known for its beautiful northern woods. The author has been able to work with state departments of natural resources, historians, arborists, and other individuals to locate the Trail Marker Trees that do remain and historical references to those that have been lost. While working with these groups the author has made countless research trips in Wisconsin. Downes, a member of the Loyal Order of the Moose, has received many helpful historical references and referrals from visiting Moose Lodges in Wisconsin and across the country. The author has also been able to show his Trail Marker Tree exhibit at public and private events in Wisconsin locations such as Boulder Junction, Minocqua, and Fence Lake Lodge.

Chapter Five

MICHIGAN

The state of Michigan is bordered by four of the five Great Lakes, giving it the longest freshwater border in the country. Michigan's location along the Great Lakes made it a prime location in the early days for the Native Americans and first Europeans. Michigan was inhabited by many Native American tribes when the first Europeans arrived including the Algonquian, Ojibwa, Potawatomi, Chippewa, and Ottawa; these tribes seemed to be some of the more prominent tribes. There were many other Native American tribes that lived in the Michigan area, such as the Miami, Menominee, Odawa, and Iroquois to name a few.

The first European to come to the Michigan area was Étienne Brûlé in the year 1620. However, the first permanent European settlement was started by Jacques Marquette much later in 1668. Michigan became an important part in the French fur trading empire; Detroit became a fur trading city and shipping post. Michigan's access to the Great Lakes allowed its inhabitants easy access to travel. The state of Michigan was involved in the lumber boom in the 1800s and 1900s; by 1869, Michigan was producing more lumber than any other state. Regrettably, similarly to the state of Wisconsin, many historic Trail Marker Trees were lost during this era of deforestation. The vast deforestation of Michigan, like Wisconsin, eventually led to increased conservation efforts. Today Michigan's land is approximately 50 percent forested land. Vacationers, nature enthusiasts, and hunters come from around the country to enjoy Michigan's thousands of miles of beaches, large forests, national and state parks, and lakes.

Although many Trail Marker Trees have been lost in Michigan due to the lumbering era and growth and development, there is early documentation that proves their existence across the state. In a 1965 article written by the Michigan Department of Conservation, Trail Marker Trees were said to still exist in Whitmore Lake, Brighton, St. Johns, Allegan, Sparta, Whitehall, Rose City, Acme, Elk Rapids, Glen Lake, Northport, Traverse City, Munising, Au Train, and Ironwood. Also in the Gogebic County History there is reference to Charles Wester's study of the Trail Marker Trees. Mr. Wester

claimed to locate 15 Trail Marker Trees in Gogebic County. The Gogebic County website states: "*Trail Marker Trees are revered as living landmarks of our pioneer past in the Gogebic County (1966)*." In the 1950s, the well-known Victor F. Lemmer wrote about Mr. Wester's efforts. Lemmer stated that there were many Indian Trail Marker Trees within the township of Ironwood and that Mr. Wester had become the authority on the subject based on his 50 year study. Although Mr. Wester's research led to a much greater awareness of the Trail Marker Trees throughout Michigan, many of his photographic examples were not authentic Trail Marker Trees. After several years of tracking down Wester's study, the author was able to review it in its entirety and unfortunately see that many of Wester's examples were far too small, thus too young, to be authentic. Also in the 1950s, Joseph Gill referenced the Trail Marker Trees in Ironwood in his published history of Gogebic County. Unfortunately, the example Gill pictured in his publication, a boxelder, was not a true Trail Marker Tree as the tree did not date back far enough. Ted Cartner, a Gogebic County resident, helped Downes locate several historic documents from the county and referred him to local historian and author Bruce Cox. Cox verified the existence of true Trail Marker Trees in the area. His uncle stated that a poor example was used by Gill, as the tree he pictured did not predate the European settlement in the area. When unrealistic examples are used to represent the Trail Marker Trees it takes credence away from the entire study and simply adds confusion. Michigan resident,

Helen Hornbeck Tanner received her Ph.D. in History from the University of Michigan and is now considered the nation's leading researcher of Native American History. In the author's most recent interview with Tanner, she stated, "*I consider the use of Trail Marker Trees common knowledge among the Native American researchers in Michigan. The bending and shaping of a tree, to simple carving or marking of the bark all conveyed messages understood by their creators.*"

Dowagiac

The city of Dowagiac is located in southern Michigan and takes its name from the Potawatomi language; Dowagiac means fishing water. Near the city of Dowagiac, Mr. Sheline, whose family had been in the Dowagiac area for four generations, brought a section of a Beech Tree from his property into the Southwestern Michigan College Museum. Upon this Beech Tree was an arborglyph of a turtle, a known Potawatomi symbol. Now in his 80s, explained that his great grandfather had been told by the local Native Americans, the Pokagon Potawatomi, the significance of this arborglyph; the tail of the turtle was pointing towards a fresh water spring that was located nearby. This ancient tree became diseased and Mr. Sheline used caution when removing it to preserve the arborglyph. Steve Arseneau, museum director, contacted the author for his expertise in regards to Native American uses of trees. There have been many historical references to the Native Americans and other cultures, such as the Basque,

Brian Winegar standing near the Howell Marker Tree during its removal. Brian Winegar and his father, George Winegar, were in charge of removing the diseased tree; they attempted to preserve as much wood from the tree as possible in order to use it to create something to commemorate the tree at a later date. Photo provided by Joyce Fisher, Archivist at the Howell Carnegie Library.

This white oak Trail Marker Tree stands northeast of Grand Rapids. Photograph provided by E. Joan Boyko, Trail Marker Tree enthusiast.

This photograph shows the monument placed by the Daughters of the American Revolution in 1923 to mark the Grand River Trail.

using tree carvings to convey messages. The bark of a beech tree once carved, will keep the same image and allow it to grow proportionately, unlike many of the hardwood species in this area. This made the beech tree the tree of choice in this area for the Native Americans, early settlers, and other cultures to use for conveying messages through carving. In the western part of the country throughout Idaho, California, and Nevada aspen trees were often used by the early Basque sheep herders to convey messages amongst themselves. J. Mallea-Olaetxe of the University of Nevada wrote the book, *Speaking through the Aspens*, discussing the Basque use of arborglyphs. The author was able to photograph the turtle arborglyph and document the information provided by Mr. Sheline.

St. Joseph

The city of St. Joseph is located along the shores of Lake Michigan in southern Michigan. Longtime friend of the author George Joseph was visiting friends, Jeff Preston and Janet Davies, at their property outside of St. Joseph. While on a hike on the property he noticed a unique tree. Mr. Joseph recognized this tree to look very similar to the many Trail Marker Tree photos that the author had shown him throughout the years. Mr. Joseph contacted Downes about this tree and Downes was also able to speak with Janet Davies, they set a date to meet at his current Trail Marker Tree exhibit in Chicago when she returned to the city. Downes was able to show Janet the exhibit and explain to her the concept

of the Trail Marker Trees. After this first meeting, the author and his wife would visit Mr. Preston and Ms. Davies at their property in Michigan to examine the Trail Marker Tree that Mr. Joseph had located. During this trip, their two boys, Jack and Chris, accompanied them to visit the Trail Marker Tree. Since this chance meeting, Ms. Davies has been very supportive of the author and his Trail Marker Tree study.

Royal Oak

This small city is a suburb of Detroit and was part of the original Saginaw Trail. The Saginaw Trail was an American Indian foot trail that led from Detroit to Saginaw; there are still visible remnants of this trail that can be seen along its route. The original trail passed through Royal Oak, Birmingham, Pontiac, Clarkston, and Flint. In the book, *Captain Streeter Pioneer*, the Michigan-born George Wellington Streeter, recalls seeing the Native Americans pass through Flint on their way to Detroit along the old Indian Trail in his early years. In 1818, the Michigan Territorial Government approved a project for a road to be built along the trail. The route of this road has been changed from the original trail. In the publication, *Royal Oak, Michigan: The Early Years*, by Owen A. Perkins, coordinator of Historical Research of the Royal Oak Historical Society, a Royal Oak Trail Marker Tree is documented. This old Trail Marker Tree was located by "Girl Scout Hill" and was believed to be a marker along the Saginaw Trail. This tree was visited by Girl Scouts and school children

This directional Trail Marker Tree is located in the Muskegon area near Bear Lake. Photo taken by the author.

This ancient double trunk Trail Marker Tree was saved by the local resident of Fruitport; it bears a strong resemblance to a well-known Trail Marker Tree in New York. Photo taken by Patrick Downes.

This directional Trail Marker Tree is located less than a mile from the other known Muskegon Trail Marker Tree. Photo taken by Gail Spreen.

for decades, where they were taught about the Trail Marker Trees and their use by the Native Americans.

Howell, Farmington, and Southfield

The city of Howell is located just west of Royal Oak. Howell was located along an Native American trail that was later referred to by the Europeans as the Grand River Trail. In 1923, the Daughters of the American Revolution commemorated this trail with a plaque mounted on a large bolder that was inscribed, "Old Indian Trail." Along this trail there were two well-known Marker Trees that stood in close proximity to each other. Both of these trees were ash and over 200 years old when they were taken down. Unfortunately, both trees have been removed due to the Emerald Ash Borer disease. The author first learned about these trees during a fundraiser he participated in at Navy Pier put on by the Catholic Charities of the Archdiocese of Chicago, The Spirit of America. A group of nuns from the Michigan area that were attending the event, told Downes about these two Marker Trees in Howell after seeing his Trail Marker Tree exhibit. Nearly a year later, Downes was contacted by a Trail Marker Tree enthusiast from the Grand Rapids area, E. Joan Boyko, after she visited his educational Trail Marker Tree website. Joan informed the author that the one remaining Marker Tree in Howell was going to be removed. With the help of Pam Rietsch, historian and Life Member of the Howell Area Chamber of Commerce, Downes and his assistant were able to get more information

This massive Trail Marker Tree stands alongside a road northeast of Grand Rapids. Photograph provided by E. Joan Boyko, Trail Marker Tree enthusiast.

about this tree and were put in contact with Joyce Fisher. Fisher is the Howell Carnegie Library Archivist and she was able to provide the author with some historical information about the two Marker Trees in Howell. These two Marker Trees were identically shaped and stood along the Grand River Trail for more than two centuries. The owner of the property where the recently removed Marker Tree once stood asked that 15 feet of the trunk be left standing. The property owner planned to have this remaining part of the Marker Tree carved to honor its significance.

Nearby, also along the Grand River Trail is the city of Farmington. A unique Trail Marker Tree used by the Potawatomi Indians stood in the city of Farmington. This unique Trail Marker Tree was shaped similarly to the letter 'U' or 'Y' and was said to stand along one of the many Native American Trails that passed through the area. The Grand River Trail, the Orchard Lake Trail, and the Shiawassee Trail all passed through this area. The Farmington Library mentions this tree on their website dedicated to the history of Farmington. The author was contacted by Stacy French regarding a possible Trail Marker Tree near the city of Southfield, which is located just east of Farmington. Stacy lived in the Lake Forest, Illinois area for 10 years where she first learned about the Trail Marker Trees. This possible Trail Marker Tree looks very similar to the unique 'U' or 'Y' shaped Trail Marker Tree used by the Potawatomi in the Farmington area. While in contact with the author, Stacy also spoke with the Southfield Historical Society about Trail Marker Trees in the Southfield area.

The Historical Society, with input from the city's forestry department, verified that Trail Marker Trees stood in the Southfield area in the past.

Grand Rapids

The city of Grand Rapids is located along an old American Indian Trail that leads from Detroit to Grand Haven. Grand Rapids is rich in Native American History and was a popular fur trading post. E. Joan Boyko, a Trail Marker Tree enthusiast, lives just northeast of Grand Rapids and has a white oak Trail Marker Tree still standing on her property. This directional Trail Marker Tree stands upon the second highest ridge in the county and appears to be leading to a nearby natural spring. Joan also located a maple Trail Marker Tree approximately three miles away from the tree that stand on her property. This massive directional Trail Marker Tree may soon perish due to the recent road improvement project that removed a section of the trees roots. Joan has been working to protect and preserve these Trail Marker Trees in her area and throughout the state. An early reference to the Native Americans using elm trees for directional purposes appeared in *The Yesterdays of Grand Rapids* by Charles E. Belknap, 1922. In this book, Belknap mentioned the Native Americans bending elm trees to indicate direction and later, the similar use of the trees by surveyors. Belknap also refers to a giant elm that was used by sailors to mark the way to Black Lake in northern Michigan, before there was a pier and channel lights.

BEHOLD THIS TREE!
— BENT BY INDIANS —
GUIDE POST ON TRAIL
DETROIT TO STRAITS OF MACKINAW

THIS MEMORIAL ERECTED BY
GRAND TRAVERSE HISTORICAL SOCIETY

This plaque is placed near the unique Trail Marker Tree to commemorate its significance. Photo provided by E. Joan Boyko.

This unique Trail Marker Tree located in Traverse City resembles many similarly shaped Trail Marker Trees found along the North Shore in Illinois. Photo provided by E. Joan Boyko.

Primary Guide of The Children's House Montessori School, Jennifer Harris, and her son meeting Dennis at a Traverse City Park.

Dennis stands behind one of the protected directional Trail Marker Trees in Traverse City.

The author standing next to one of the Marker Trees of this remarkable Council Circle.

This historic sign can be found on the property of the Greensky Hill Mission. This sign mentions the new Council Circle created to commemorate the original Council Circle that the author was able to locate with the help of the property owners and locals.

pages 172–173
This photograph shows three Marker Trees making part of the Council Circle. These maple trees are identically shaped and equally spaced creating a perfect circle.

Fruit Port, Muskegon, and Twin Lake

Further west along the old Indian Trail, along what today is Highway 96, near the village of Fruitport is an ancient Trail Marker Tree. This double trunk Trail Marker Tree was saved by the people of Fruitport; they ensured the tree was unharmed during the building of Highway 96. Just north of Fruitport, in the area of Muskegon, are two directional Trail Marker Trees. The author was able to locate these two trees, as well as the Trail Marker Tree in Fruitport, with the help of Elizabeth Sherman. Elizabeth Sherman is a historian, author, and host of the historic Langeland House Bed and Breakfast. She assisted Downes over a number of years, not only helping him locate the Trail Marker Trees, but also sharing information about the history of the trees and the area. Throughout this area there has been a strong effort to preserve these historical landmarks left behind by the Ottawa and Potawatomi Indians.

Owasippe Scout Reservation is located in Twin Lake, just north of Muskegon. Owasippe is the oldest Boy Scout camp in America, and at one point, the reservation covered 11,000 acres. The author was told about Trail Marker Trees on the Owasippe property by an Antioch resident Eagle Scout. Downes made a trip to the reservation to locate the trees with his wife and Brian and Nadean Buchholz. The Owasippe staff was very helpful and interested in the Trail Marker Trees. Unfortunately, they were not able to locate the trees during this trip. The author provided photos and educational brochures to the

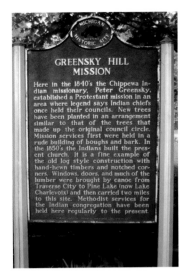

staff to help educate the Boy Scouts at this camp about the history of the Trail Marker Trees. Downes plans to return to the reservation and attempt to locate the Trail Marker Trees in the future.

Traverse City, Charlevoix, and Harbor Springs

Traverse City is located along the West Arm of the Grand Traverse Bay. There are many Trail Marker Trees the Traverse City area, and today, there are two trees that have been protected by the locals. One unique Trail Marker Tree is located on private property off of Washington Street and is commemorated with a plaque. This tree was referenced in the book, *Michigan: A Guide to the Wolverine State*, by the Federal Writer's Project in 1941: "*A living reminder of Indian days is the deformed Trail-Marker Tree, east of the courthouse on the north side of Washington St., which follows the old trail.*" E. Joan Boyko of Grand Rapids brought this Trail Marker Tree to the author's attention, after which he was able to locate several old references to this tree. This Trail Marker Tree bears a strong resemblance to the uniquely formed Trail Marker Trees mentioned throughout the North Shore area in Illinois. Another Trail Marker Tree in the Traverse City area is located in the Traverse City Park near the Civic Center. This directional Trail Marker Tree is one of two that stood in that park; the other tree is no longer standing. Jennifer Harris used to work with the author and is currently a teacher at The Children's House, an Independent Montessori School.

While Jennifer was working with the author she wrote a poem, "A Tree and a Man." She gave this poem to the author and it has since been read by thousands. Jennifer located this Trail Marker Tree while visiting and hiking through the park.

North of Traverse City in the Charlevoix area is the Greensky Hill Mission. This Christian Mission was founded in the 1800s by a Chippewa (Ojibwe) Chief, Peter Greensky, and had many Chippewa members. This northern area of Michigan is also known for its history with the Odawa and Ottawa Indians. According to legend, near the Greensky Hill Mission there was a circle of "council trees" where the Native American chiefs would meet and discuss important issues and hold ceremonies.

In the 1990s Downes was contacted by a Michigan artist, Ladislav Hanka, after he had visited Downes' site. Hanka told Downes about the legend of this Council Circle and recommended he research the Charlevoix area to find more information. The author was able to locate the Greensky Hill Mission and view a newer Council Circle that was formed to commemorate the original Council Circle; this newer circle of trees is not nearly old enough to have been formed during the time the Native Americans lived in the area. However, after speaking with several locals, Downes was able to locate the original Council Circle. This revered Council Circle has been formed by identically shaped maple trees creating a perfect circle. Based on the diameters of all of the included trees, this Council Circle was formed approximately 200 years ago. In this unique Council Circle, all of the trees were bent outwardly

This photograph shows an interesting cluster of shaped trees. Outdoor enthusiasts Candis Collick and Coni Craig originally thought these trees to be Trail Marker Trees, but with further research discovered they were shaped in the 1940's by the DNR for the native Grouse population. Photo provided by Candis Collick and Coni Craig.

The photograph was discovered by the author while researching Trail Marker Trees in Michigan. The photograph was taken in 1956 in Hales Corners, Wisconsin, just outside of Muskego. This enormous tree is similarly shaped to the uniquely shaped Trail Marker Trees known to have been used by the Potawatomi. Photo courtesy of the Victor Lemmer papers, Box2, Bentley Historical Library, University of Michigan.

at about 10 feet from the ground, creating a flowing uniformity throughout the circle. The locals that know about the Council Circle have had information about it passed onto them from earlier generations.

The Odawa Indians were said to have originally formed this Council Circle. The author felt very privileged to be able to witness such a magnificent landmark of the past. The owner of the property where the Council Circle is located gave the author permission to document and photograph these trees. Out of respect for the Odawa and the other Indian Tribes that used this Council Circle, the local residents hope to keep its location private to help protect and preserve these trees for generations to come.

North of Charlevoix along the Little Traverse Bay is the city of Harbor Springs. The area of Harbor Springs was a French mission originally named Arbre Croche, the French words for Crooked Tree. According to a publication written in 1887 by Andrew J. Blackbird, when the Ottawa Indians first came to this area, they saw a large and very crooked pine tree on the shore of Traverse Bay. The Ottawa called it, "Waw-gaw-naw-ke-zee," meaning "crooked top of tree." The pine tree became known as a landmark for the area. This story about this tree was also included in the Traditional Ojibway Resources in the Western Great Lakes, by the Bureau of Applied Research in Anthropology, the University of Arizona. This crooked pine tree is a great example of a Marker Tree that was used first by the Native Americans and then by the European settlers to help locate the area.

This photograph, also taken in 1956, shows the sign installed next to the Trail Marker Tree to commemorate its significance. This tree was authenticated by the Officials of the Milwaukee Public Museum. This photograph and the photograph of the tree itself were kept on file by Victor F. Lemmer, a Michigan author and historian. Photo courtesy of the Victor Lemmer papers, Box2, Bentley Historical Library, University of Michigan.

INDIAN TRAIL MARKER TREE

You are standing on what was once a major Indian Trail that led thru deep, stretches of unbroken forests to the shores of Lake Michigan. The large Elm, with the unique jog in the trunk, is an authentic Indian Trail Marker Tree. There are only a few isolated specimens of this type in all Wisconsin. This is the nearest to Milwaukee.

The trail ran parallel to the jog, which points southwesterly, indicating the way to big Muskego Lake where there were numerous camp sites in prehistoric times and the Potawatomi had several villages in historic times.

The Indians would nick & break a sapling at a right angle to vertical growth & parallel to the trail.

The sapling would grow in this position for a while & then renew it's upward growth. In this particular tree, the original trunk of the sapling continued it's growth upward, even after the Breaking, thereby restricting the growth of the horizontal limb.

This tree is over 60 feet tall and is probably over 200 years old. It is here today as living evidence of the Indian Lore of yesteryear.

Authenticated by Officials of The Milwaukee Public Museum

A Tree and a Man

You, of indigenous past,
dark and wrinkled,
as flesh of time,
of sun,
take root.

To last for lives,
spin your rings
like spool and spider.

Root in these eastern
woodlands,
to point a knotty finger
to the river,
to the sacred,
to the home.

Stretched in youth
by strap of hide,
pulled tightly to earth, as braid.

Your arm, your limb,
raised to grow and run,
like footpath beneath,

carry me, once more,
through starless night,
through snow underfoot,
through times of sky,
blackened by storm.

And you, with walking
stick and gentle hand,
you are passage, and this
before us, preservation.

Chosen to teach,
the window of the past,
pained with trail and
trespass.

You have listened,
and learned as child with
curious mind,
amongst the elders of oak
and elm.

In soil rich with rain,
you hunt and gather
those unearthed elements.

You search for meaning,
for history within these
ancient natures.

So that you, as those before,
may come together,
sparked by festival of fire,
to bare truth and to bare trade.

Jennifer Harris

Northern Michigan

The Mackinaw area in northern Michigan was well known as a central destination for the fur trade. Before its development as a center for the fur trade, this area in northern Michigan was inhabited and traveled by many Native American tribes because of its location amidst the Great Lakes. The nearby area of Mackinac was referred to over a century ago by Dr. Frank Grover in his paper, *Some Indian Land Marks of the North Shore*, because of the Trail Marker Trees that existed throughout the vicinity.

Outdoor enthusiasts Candis Collick and Coni Craig contacted the author about several possible Trail Marker Trees on Drummond Island in northern Michigan. These Trail Marker Tree enthusiasts had located several unique trees in the Glen Cove area of Drummond Island, including a few clusters of trees. Downes recommended that Candis and Coni obtain more information, such as circumference and species of the possible Trail Marker Trees. Candis and Coni continued to research the trees, they obtaining measurements and verifying the species of the trees. With this information they were able to determine the trees' approximate age. These trees were all only around 50 to 60 years old, making it impossible for them to be authentic Trail Marker Trees. However, their research led to the discovery that these trees were in fact shaped by the DNR in the 1940s as part of a project dealing with the native Grouse population's habitat. These women's solid and dedicated research was a great example of how research should be conducted regarding the Trail Marker Trees. Unfortunately,

not every misshapen tree is a Marker or Trail Marker Tree, and before identifying a tree as an authentic Trail Marker Tree, certain factual information should be obtained. Candis and Coni discovered an interesting bit of more recent history about Drummond Island and continue to be Trail Marker Tree enthusiasts.

Another island in the northernmost part of Michigan, Manitou Island, has been documented as having a Trail Marker Tree. Most recently in the 1990s, Rita Hadra Rusco mentioned a specific Trail Marker Tree in her book, *North Manitou Island-Between Sunrise and Sunset*. Downes also plans to further research this tree and verify its authenticity as a Trail Marker Tree. The author also plans an upcoming research trip to the Crystal Falls area in the Upper Peninsula. Professor Emeritus of Ojibwe, Earl R. Otchingwanigan, of the Minnesota State University, contacted the author regarding two possible Trail Marker Trees in Iron County, Michigan. Earl Otchingwanigan's primary concern is the preservation of the Trail Marker Trees and other remnants of the Ojibwe Culture. Both of these possible Trail Marker Trees are located along a trail that led from a known Ojibwe village on Chicaugon Lake.

The state of Michigan is truly unique due to its location bordering four of the five Great Lakes. When the American Indians and early settlers lived in the area, access to the Great Lakes would have provided them with many natural resources and the advantage of travel by water. While the author has conducted over 30 research trips in and throughout Michigan locating and educating the public about Trail Marker Trees, he believes there could be many more undocumented trees still to be found.

Chapter Six

ONTARIO

The Canadian province of Ontario borders the
Great Lakes Region in the United States. This vast province
has a beautiful and varied landscape with endless
lakes and rivers, making it a wilderness paradise for the
outdoor enthusiast.

This sketch represents a grafted Sugar Maple that was said to be formed by the Iroquois and was located near Lake Ontario. Sketch submitted by Paul O'Hara.

The author researching pictographs at the famous Agawa Rock in the Lake Superior Provincial Park located in between Sault Ste. Marie and Wawa. Photo taken by Gail Spreen.

This ancient white oak trail marker tree is located on an old Indian trail that is documented by a surveyor's map from 1790. It is protected now by a private golf and country club in Kingsville, Ontario. Paul Lemieux is the gentleman standing next to the tree. Photo by Paul O'Hara.

A documented pictograph of a grafted tree was found in a cave located in LaMoille Minnesota. The book: *The Aborigines of Minnesota, A Report Based on the Collections of Jacob V. Brower, and on the Filed Surveys and Notes of Alfred J. Hill and Theodore H. Lewis*, Published by the Minnesota Historical Society in 1911.

This ancient grafted cedar tree is located in the Forbidden City in China. Photograph taken by the author.

The author and his wife, Gail, at the Kinniwabi Pines Restaurant overlooking the Michipicoten River near Wawa with outdoor guides and resort owners Klaus and Wilma Brauer.

The author's late Uncle John spent quite a bit of time in the Lake of the Woods area in the 1930s, navigating through the wilderness on foot and by canoe. The stories Uncle John related to Dennis initially sparked his interest in the vast wilderness areas in Ontario. Downes has since traveled to all of the southern Canadian provinces searching for Marker and Trail Marker Trees. Throughout the course of these many research trips, the author has had the opportunity to talk with professionals in the forestry field and form friendships with outdoor hunting and fishing guides. In his more recent trips, Downes had the opportunity to spend time with the late Klaus Brauer, an experienced outdoorsman and guide, and his equally experienced wife, Wilma. Currently, there are few documented Trail Marker Trees in Canada. As with many of the Great Lakes states, the Canadian provinces near waterways were heavily logged, which led to the demise of many Trail Marker Trees near the navigable waterways. However, the author hopes as more people become knowledgeable about the trees, living examples will be discovered in the many remote areas throughout Canada.

During many of the author's research trips, he was able to study the well documented rock art throughout the Canadian Shield region. This rock art, commonly called pictographs, has been traced back thousands of years by archeologists. These pictographs could have been used to aid in navigation by providing references and direction to those who could under-stand their meaning. The Cree and Ojibwe people have been credited with creating this expansive rock art. The author

learned much about pictographs created by Native Americans in the Canadian Shield region by reading old texts written by Henry Schoolcraft. Schoolcraft also referred to the American Indians' practice of carving into and painting on trees to convey messages and aid in navigation. He specifically discussed the well-known Arbre Croche, the crooked tree used by the Native Americans and Europeans to locate a village from the water.

Canada, like the United States, had numerous Native American tribes living within its borders. Specific to the Ontario area were the Iroquois, the Algonquin, the Huron, the Cree, the Ottawa, the Ojibwe, the Neutral, and the Delaware. Throughout the southern provinces of Canada there were many well-known paths and trails, most of which were originally formed by the Native Americans. One of the best known trails in Ontario is the Humber Portage, also known as the Toronto Carrying-Place Trail. This trail connected Toronto to Lake Simcoe using the Humber River as one of its navigational references. The Native Americans in Ontario primarily navigated along the shores of the many bodies of water making the port towns like Sault Ste. Marie and Wawa important meeting places. These port towns continued to gain prominence during the Fur Trade Era. In the northern parts of Canada, the Inuit were the most common indigenous people. The ancient Inuit used a special form of marker to navigate their arctic lands; called the Inuksuit. The Inuksuit was a single upright stone that would tower above the barren landscape or was created by stacking unworked stones into a similar monument. A related stone monument, the Inunnguaq, was created in the form of a man. Like the Trail Marker Trees, these ancient markers were used for marking trails.

Just as the Native Americans used special grafted trees as Markers along bodies of water in the United States, they also used the grafted trees along bodies of water in Canada. Paul O'Hara, a botanist and landscape designer, sent Downes a sketch of a grafted tree that was located near Lake Ontario. O'Hara also located possible Trail Marker Trees throughout the southern Ontario area. Two of the trees that O'Hara located are approximately 400 meters apart along a trail; both trees appear to be pointing towards Lake Ontario. The author hopes to verify the authenticity of these possible Trail Marker Trees in the near future.

Centuries ago, North America was a very different place. Throughout Ontario and the Great Lakes states, there were massive and untouched forests, vast grasslands taller than any man, and perilous swamps. There were many dangers that could be encountered from poisonous snakes and disease carrying mosquitos to grizzly bears, cougars, and enemies from rival tribes. However, these lands also provided every natural resource imaginable for the Native Americans. Navigating safely to locate these resources became a matter of life and death, making navigational aids, like the Trail Marker Trees or the Inuksuit, a way to increase survival.

Chapter Seven

INDIANA

Indiana boasts a most unusual and varied terrain from the famous sand dunes, to mysterious caverns and caves, to treacherous swamplands, and even ancient forests. Indiana was part of the Northwest Territory, the first western frontier. In the early 1540s, explorer Hernando de Soto described the swamps in Indiana as worse than what he had seen in all of Florida.

Today, many of the swamps have been drained and filled to allow construction, but the sand dunes and portions of the ancient forests have been preserved. The Native Americans, and later, the Europeans, were drawn to the area of Indiana because of the access to the Great Lakes, major rivers running through the area, plentiful wild game, large prairies of wild grasses for the buffalo herds, swamps and marshes that were teaming with waterfowl, and rich soil for cultivating. There were many Native American tribes that inhabited the area of Indiana including the Miami, Potawatomi, Piankashaw, Shawnee, Illini, Delaware, Kickapoo, and others. One of the early cultures, the Middle Mississippian Culture, left behind the Angel Mounds. Today this historical site is one of the most well preserved in the country. The Angel Mounds were inhabited from approximately 1100 A.D. to 1450 A.D. As with many of the Great Lakes states, Indiana had many trails crisscrossing its land. One of the most famous trails, the Vincennes Trace, ran from Vincennes to Chicago. Another famous trail that led from the Mississippi River in Illinois, through Indiana, and on to the Detroit River in Michigan was the Sauk Trail. Even with the few main trails that led through the area, navigation was very difficult and explorers often found themselves lost. In the book, *Historic Highways of America, Volume 8*, the author quoted notes that were taken during George Rogers Clark's explorations in Indiana. One such quote read, "*...There is danger of being bewildered, as happened to one of my fellow travellers, three years before, when, with two others, he roamed*

about for seventeen days." Clark was referred to as the Conqueror of the Old Northwest; most of his explorations in this area were in the late 1770s.

The people of Indiana have worked to protect their ancient and historical sites. The Prairie Club of Chicago, founded in 1908 by Henry Cowles, Thomas Allinson, and Jens Jensen, helped to save the Indiana sand dunes from commercial interests. The Daughters of the American Revolution marked several areas of historical significance to both the American Indians and the early Europeans throughout the 1930s. In 1934, the DAR placed a large boulder with a bronze plaque at the corner of Berry and Clay Streets to mark the site of General Anthony Wayne's fort. The plaque reads: "*The site of General Anthony Wayne's Fort dedicated Oct 22, 1794. It was the first United States Fort near "Three Rivers." This fort commanded the shortest portage between the St. Lawrence and Mississippi systems, a portage known to the Indians as "Glorious Gate" and a strategic crossroads in early trade and exploration. Presented to the city of Fort Wayne by the Indiana Daughters of the American Revolution, April 6, 1934.*"

Indiana's history of the Trail Marker Trees has been well documented over the years. By the mid 1930s, Dr. Raymond Janssen had already documented several Trail Marker Trees in Indiana. Today, historical societies, groups, and individuals are still working to preserve these important parts of their history.

The author has worked with several local historians throughout Indiana. Judith Baker, director of the White County

previous page

Greg Prochnow, Judith Baker, and local historian posed behind the ancient Trail Marker Tree in Buffalo Indiana. This tree is estimated to be over 350 years old. Photo taken by the author.

The author and White County Historical Society Director, Judith Baker, measuring and documenting the "Grandfather" Trail Marker Tree. Photo taken by Greg Prochnow.

The second remaining Trail Marker Tree in Monon in White County, also estimated to be over 350 years old. Photo taken by Greg Prochnow.

This photograph shows another of the uniquely shaped Trail Marker Trees known to be formed by the Potawatomi. Photo taken by Judith Baker.

Downes pictured next to the massive Treaty Tree. Photo taken by Judith Baker.

following page left

A photo of the same Monon Trail Marker Tree taken in 1948. Photo courtesy of the White County Historical Society.

following page right

This photo, taken in the 1940's, shows a Trail Marker Tree that stood in Newton Township and was said to mark the trail that lead to an Indian village along the Kankakee. Photo courtesy of the White County Historical Society.

Historical Society, was very instrumental in the author's
Trail Marker Tree research in Indiana. Downes has
conducted numerous research trips to Indiana during the
course of his study. Baker not only helped the author locate
historical references, but she also accompanied him on many
research trips to document living Trail Marker Trees. Much
of the early research about the Trail Marker Trees in White
County was conducted by Marilyn Abbott. According to
Madden and Dold in the *175th Anniversary of White County*,
Marilyn was considered to be a tireless researcher and a
strong voice for the White County Historical Society; she was
a champion of historic preservation. Marilyn documented
many White County and surrounding area Trail Marker Trees,
creating maps and notes that are still on file at the White
County Historical Museum. Through Marilyn's research
and other historical references, Baker was able to provide the
author with valuable information.

Just off of the Tippecanoe River in Buffalo, one of the
grandest examples of a living Trail Marker Trees is located.
A Native American, living in White County, Buffalo Heart
was interviewed by a local newspaper regarding her
knowledge of the Trail Marker Trees. Buffalo Heart refers
specifically to this ancient tree as 'Grandfather' out of respect
for the tree and its significance to her people. Buffalo Heart
remembers numerous Trail Marker Trees located throughout
White County from her childhood. Unfortunately, many of
these trees have been cut down or removed for housing

developments, roads, and other construction projects. During her interview she refers to two remaining Trail Marker Trees in White County and her desire to protect them by not disclosing their exact locations. The other remaining Trail Marker Tree is located in Monon; both of these trees were photographically documented in the 1940s. Historians in the area believe that these two trees led to a nearby exposed copper deposit. Luckily, both trees are located on private property and the property owners are helping to protect these trees into the future. The author was able to visit and document both of these remaining Trail Marker Trees with the help of the White County Historical Society and the permission of the individual property owners.

Nearby, there is a locally famous Marker Tree commemorated by the 1836 Treaty between the Potawatomi and the United States government. This tree, referred to as the Treaty Tree, is located northeast of Buffalo along the Chippewanung Creek. This enormous tree has been well documented and preserved throughout its history. The Treaty Tree is located on private property, arrangements were made for the author to accompany local historian, Judith Baker, to the site in order to document this distinctive Marker Tree.

South of White County, near the town of Lafayette, is a unique Trail Marker Tree similar to the Trail Marker Trees found throughout northern Illinois known to be shaped by the Potawatomi. Judith Baker was informed of this tree by other local historians, including L.A. Clugh. Downes, accompanied by Baker, visited many historical locations in and around Lafayette, including the site of this Trail Marker Tree. After the author's last research trip to Indiana, he was contacted by a Trail Marker Tree enthusiast, Mr. Sattler, from the Lafayette area. Mr. Sattler informed Downes about a possible Trail Marker Tree located in his backyard; coincidentally his property is located off of Bent Tree Court. This possible Trail Marker Tree is located atop of a ravine and is pointing downwards towards Indian Creek. The tree is over three feet in diameter, making it approximately 280 years old. The author has been unable to document this tree in person, but plans to verify its authenticity in the near future.

The city of South Bend Indiana had a large historic oak, referred to as the Council Oak, that stood until 1992. Under the Council Oak, the French Explorer LaSalle met with the Miami and Illinois Indians to sign a treaty in 1681. A large boulder and bronze plaque were placed by the Council Oak to commemorate its historical significance by a local historical society. In the 1960s, long before this massive oak was removed due to disease and an unfortunate lightning strike, a local teacher was said to have planted an acorn from this tree nearby and named it the "Council Oak Jr." Today, the large boulder and bronze plaque can still been seen at the site of the Council Oak. The interest and dedication of local Indiana residents and historians have helped to preserve the history of the area Marker and Trail Marker Trees.

Chapter Eight

MISSOURI

The state of Missouri took its name from the Missouri River, named by the early Native Americans living in the area. Originally, when the first Europeans came to the Missouri area, it was inhabited by the Miami, Illini, Osage, Delaware, Kickapoo, Piankashaw, Shawnee, and others.

Missouri's capital city of St. Louis can be found at the confluence of two great river systems, the Missouri and Mississippi. These two river systems would have provided great resources and convenient travel for Missouri's early inhabitants. The lower half of Missouri is covered by the beautiful Ozarks, a mountainous and forested area known for its breathtaking lakes. The state is also home to more than 6,000 caves, second only to Tennessee. The combination of the rivers, forests, and caves provided great resources for Missouri's earliest inhabitants. Today, these areas provide opportunities for hiking, boating, spelunking, and simply admiring natural beauty for all varieties of tourists.

There have been numerous Marker and Trail Marker Trees reported throughout the state of Missouri. Some of these trees have been authenticated as actual Native American Trail Marker Trees, whereas, other examples have been studied and found to be too young to be authentic Trail Marker Trees.

The author has documented several authentic Trail Maker Trees throughout the state based on a number of research trips and collaboration with arborists and Native American historical experts.

On the far western side of the state, near Kansas City, there is an impressive example of a double trunk Trail Marker Tree on one of the oldest homesteads in the area. Here, in Tiffany Springs, this oak Trail Marker Tree marks the nearby spring. The property owner, Ralph, and his wife have owned and maintained the property for decades. In the early 1970s, a Trail Marker Tree enthusiast visited this tree and informed Ralph of its historical

significance. Since then, Ralph has ensured that no harm come to this tree. Downes was able to measure and document this tree with Ralph's permission.

Due west of Tiffany Springs, in the city of Fayette, there is a massive Trail Marker Tree located upon a hill and clearly visible from the surrounding areas. This directional Trail Marker Tree is over 300 years old and still appears strong and healthy. Arborist Brian Buchholz and the author believe this tree led to a safe crossing point on the nearby Missouri River. This ancient Trail Marker Tree has been visited and documented by Missouri Trail Marker Tree enthusiasts over the past several decades.

Continuing east across the state, near the city of Warrenton, the author was informed about a possible Trail Marker Tree by Scott Holmes. Holmes first learned about the Trail Marker Trees when he hosted the author's Trail Marker Tree exhibit at his shop and gallery in Wilmot, Wisconsin. Downes was able to locate this directional Trail Marker Tree with directions from Holmes; he photographed and documented it. Just east of Warrenton, in the city of Lake St. Louis, there is a double trunk Trail Marker Tree. This tree was recognized by the Federated Garden Clubs of Missouri, and they installed a small sign to help commemorate the tree. Greg Prochnow, who frequently travels with the author on research trips, was informed about the tree by a friend, Lynn, who had lived in the nearby Bent Oak Apartments. With the information from Lynn, Downes and Prochnow were able to locate and

document the large double trunk Trail Marker Tree. This tree still stands today off of the road named in its honor, Bent Oak Drive. The author was able to contact Jean Roseman, president of the Federated Garden Clubs of Missouri, about this tree and previous research conducted in the state regarding the Trail Marker Trees. Laura Hubler, once a member of the Garden Club, was a Trail Marker Tree enthusiast and helped to bring awareness about the trees to the state of Missouri in the 1970's and early 1980's.

South of the St. Louis area, near the Fort Leonard Wood and Mark Twain Forest area, there have been many Trail Marker Trees reported. The author was contacted by Mike Walker, Directorate of Environmental Integration for the U.S. Army Engineer School. Walker had located several Trail Marker Trees on the Fort Leonard Wood base and invited Downes to view the trees. Walker has written several articles about the Trail Marker Trees in the area of southern Missouri. The author could not verify all of the trees Walker had located as being authentic Trail Marker Trees. However, some of these trees were authentic based on age and shape. The articles Walker has written have helped to bring awareness about these historical trees to the people in Missouri. Downes' cousin, Tarik Jensen, is currently located at the Fort Leonard Wood base and has visited some of the living Trail Marker Trees. Just outside of Fort Leonard Wood in Dixon, there is a double trunk Trail Marker Tree that points in the direction of a nearby spring and a cave. Bridgette Purcell contacted the author about this

Dennis near the two largest remaining oaks at the Cedar Creek location.

This double trunk Trail Marker Tree is located near Dixon. Photo submitted by Bridgette Purcell.

Arborist, Brian Buchholz, examining two of the smaller modified trees at the Cedar Creek location.

This is another Trail Marker Tree located near the Fort Leonard Wood area; this photo was sent to the author by historian and Trail Marker Tree enthusiast Linda Gardner Phillips.

Arborist, Brian Buchholz, and Native American Historical Expert, Knonozo, standing near an unusual triple trunk oak at the Cedar Creek location. Photo taken by the author.

tree, and with her photographs and measurements of the tree, it is estimated this tree is approximately 200 years old.

Along the southern border of the state near the Roaring River Conservation Area, there are two Trail Marker Trees located side by side. One of the trees is a single trunk directional Trail Marker Tree and the other is a double trunk Trail Marker Tree. According to Potawatomi Historical Expert, Knonozo, when two Trail Marker Trees were located in such close proximity, it would provide more information to the Native American, a special message that would be understood by those who shaped the trees. Similar examples have been recorded in nearby states, including Wisconsin and Illinois. Arborist Brian Buchholz accompanied the author to photograph and document these two Trail Marker Trees.

With the help of local Native Americans, Laura Hubler located a unique cluster of trees modified by mankind near Cedar Creek. Hubler referred to this cluster of modified trees as the Quilting Party. All eight of the original modified trees in this location were white oak and were modified in different ways. Some of the trees appeared to look like the directional Trail Marker Trees, while others had two or three upright limbs. The author has visited this site on three separate occasions with an Native American historical expert and arborists. Downes determined that although some of these trees could be old enough to date back to the times of the Native American, others that were less than 10 inches in diameter were more likely shaped by people visiting the site much later. The few trees that do remain at this site are in demise, and it is apparent

An example of a directional Trail Marker Tree along a known Indian trail. This Trail Marker Tree had an additional and unwanted branch sprout up from the trunk after the Native Americans left the area and ceased tending to the tree. The author has noticed the appearance of these additional branches on the trees he has shaped over the decades.

Another example of Trail Marker Trees Dennis located in the state of Missouri.

Downes researching the area caves near a Trail Marker Tree site. This is one of thousands of caves found throughout the state of Missouri. Photo taken by Brian Buchholz.

The author standing near the set of two Trail Marker Trees located near the Roar River Conservation Area. Photo taken by Brian Buchholz.

that some of these trees have been vandalized. The author believes the misconception of these trees as treasure trees has led to much of this vandalism; treasure seekers carving into and digging around these trees to locate a nonexistent treasure have caused significant damage to these historical landmarks here and across the country.

Hubler initially learned about the Trail Marker Trees in Illinois as a young girl. After retirement, she and her husband moved to Missouri, where she regained an interest in the trees and contacted several Illinois historical societies to collect more information about the trees she had seen as a child. Much of the information Hubler collected came from the research of Dr. Raymond Janssen, a life-long Illinois resident. Using this information, Hubler searched for Trail Marker Trees throughout the state of Missouri. She located some excellent examples of living Trail Marker Trees as well as some examples that were later called into question by the United States Forest Service. In 1970, the Forest Service took core samples from several trees Hubler identified as Trail Marker Trees to determine an approximate age at her request. The Forest Service was able to determine that many of the trees examined were less than 100 years old, and some were less than 50 years old. Although all of her examples were not authenticated, Hubler spent a great amount of time raising awareness and striving to protect these Native American Trail Marker Trees. Later in life, Hubler was bestowed awards from both the Native American community and the Forestry Service for her efforts to raise awareness and protect the Trail Marker Trees.

Chapter Nine

OHIO

Some of the earliest traces of man among the Great Lakes states can be found in Ohio. The Ohio area offered the ancients a variety of natural resources, including food, shelter, wild game, and minerals. In ancient times, the Scioto Salt Licks and the Flint Ridge drew many Native Americans to the Ohio area. The Scioto Salt Licks had numerous paths from all directions leading to them, and both the animals and early man made trips to there. Other locations where salt licks were found had similar findings and remains of ancient trails.

The Flint Ridge, located in eastern Ohio, was invaluable to the Native Americans. It was nearly eight miles long and would provide flint for the Native Americans to make arrowheads, spearpoints, small knives, and other tools. Flint Ridge was also prized for its distinctive coloration; it contained various shades of flint, white, red, blue, yellow, and even green. The early Hopewell culture appeared to be responsible for the majority of the quarrying at Flint Ridge. Archeologists have found that the Hopewell culture never actually lived at the site of Flint Ridge. Thus they would have had well-marked trails and paths leading from their villages to Flint Ridge. Many of the ancient Ohio cultures were known for their incredible earthworks and effigy mounds. Some of these early documented cultures are the Adena, Hopewell, Fort Ancient People, and Whittlesey Focus People.

Two of the most notable ancient sites still protected in Ohio today are the Serpent Mound and Fort Ancient. The Serpent Mound, said to be built by the early Adena culture, became the first privately funded archaeological preserve in the United States. Frederick Putnam of the Peabody Museum and Harvard University excavated portions of the Serpent Mound in the 1880's. The Serpent Mound is 1,348 feet long and is the largest effigy mound in the country. Fort Ancient is the largest prehistoric Indian hilltop earthwork in North America. Fort Ancient was surrounded by nearly 20,000 feet of earthen walls. This site was built by the Hopewell culture, and archeologists are still uncovering new mysteries about this

ancient culture today. In 1891, Fort Ancient became the first site in the Ohio Historical Society's network of historic sites. The Hopewell culture left behind images of beaver on many stone artifacts. The beaver was a staple to the Indians, providing them with food and fur. Approximately ten thousand years ago, there were giant beavers living throughout the Till Plains of Ohio. The giant beavers, Castoroides ohioensi, would have ranged in size from 250 pounds up to 400 pounds. The first recorded remains of this giant beaver were from Nashport, Ohio. In prehistoric times, along with the giant beaver, the Native Americans would have had to contend with giant teratorns, American lions, and the short faced bear. The author has visited and researched the Serpent Mound and Fort Ancient, along with the areas surrounding them as part of his ongoing study.

There were many other documented effigy mounds and earthworks throughout Ohio. A complex network of paths and trails existed connecting many of these sites and other sites of importance. These trails also created portages between Ohio's many river systems. The Great Black Swamp covered thousands of square miles in northwestern Ohio. This vast swamp had a variety of different vegetation; it was composed of low watery meadows and higher areas of lush forests. The Black Swamp would have provided certain types of vegetation that could not be found elsewhere along with plentiful waterfowl and reptiles. However, the swamp was also treacherous in parts with waist high waters, clouds of

page 199
This photograph, taken by the author, shows a view from the tail end of the Serpent Mound that extends nearly a quarter mile to its head.

Dennis standing near the famous Serpent Mound in Peebles, Ohio.

The author researching teratorns and other prehistoric animals that the early Paleo-Indians would have encountered. This photograph was taken at the La Brea Tar Pits in California by Gail Spreen.

This plaque was placed near the Signal Tree to mark its significance.

This famous Marker Tree, locally known as the Signal Tree, marked the portage between the Cuyahoga and Tuscarawas Rivers. This enormous tree still stands today.

THE SIGNAL TREE

TREES WITH UNUSUAL SHAPES WERE OFTEN USED BY INDIANS AS LANDMARKS TO IDENTIFY IMPORTANT TRAILS. THIS 300 YEAR OLD BUR OAK (QUERCUS MACROCARPA) MARKED THE NORTHERNMOST POINT OF THE PORTAGE TRAIL, WHICH CONNECTED THE CUYAHOGA (WHOSE COURSE WAS ONCE MUCH CLOSER TO THE TREE) AND TUSCARAWAS RIVERS. THE ERIE, SENECA, SHAWNEE, OTTAWA, DELAWARE AND MINGO TRIBES TRAVELED TO THE OHIO RIVER BY THIS ROUTE. THEY REMOVED THEIR CANOES FROM THE CUYAHOGA RIVER HERE AND CARRIED THEM OVERLAND FOR EIGHT MILES--SOUTH TO SUMMIT LAKE. LATER, WHITE SETTLERS USED THE SAME SIGNAL TREE TO FIND THEIR WAY BETWEEN THE RIVERS.

-1986-

disease carrying insects, poisonous snakes, impenetrable brush, and thick impassible mud. By 1900, the Black Swamp was almost completely drained after years of efforts by state and county ditching projects. Deep drainage ditches can still be seen lining many roads in northwestern Ohio as reminders of the enormous efforts required to drain the swamp. The many ancient paths would have helped the Native Americans navigate safely through the Great Swamp.

When the Europeans arrived in the Ohio area, some of the Native American tribes that were occupying the land were the Shawnee, Delaware, Iroquois, Miami, Ottawa, Chippewa, Potawatomi, Ojibwa, and others. There were numerous Native American trails throughout Ohio that the Europeans also began using. Three of the best known Indian trails were the Great Trail, the Warrior's Trail, and the Scioto Trail. Along one of the Indian Trails, near the banks of Ohio River in the Marietta area, George Washington found a large sycamore tree that he measured to be over 40 feet in circumference. This large tree would have served as a reference point for the early Europeans as well as the Native Americans in the area. Along with this early notable Marker, there are documented Trail Marker Trees in the state of Ohio.

One of the oldest documented Marker Trees in Ohio is known locally as the Signal Tree. This tree is located near Cuyahoga Falls. It is over 300 years old and still stands along the portage trail connecting the Cuyahoga and Tuscarawas Rivers. This tree has been referred to locally for marking the

portage trail since the early 1800s. A permanent plaque has been placed by the tree to commemorate its significance to the Native Americans and early European settlers.

West of Cuyahoga Falls in the village of Woodville is another documented Trail Marker Tree. This double trunk tree marked the shallow crossing or ford of the Portage River. In 1969, the Kiwanis erected a bronze plaque to commemorate the Trail Marker Tree; the plaque was inscribed: "*Indians lived in this area until 1817. They marked forest trails by bending young trees to point the way. The ancient hackberry tree, just west of the bridge, bent when young, points to a shallow crossing of the Portage River.*" The plaque and Trail Marker Tree can still be seen at Trail Marker Park in Woodville.

On the southern end of the state near Brush Creek Township there was a Trail Marker Tree located in the Nature Conservancy, Lynx Prairie. Lynx Prairie was designated a National Landmark by the National Park Service in 1967, largely due to the efforts of Dr. E. Lucy Braun. Dr. Braun was a Professor of Ecology in the Department of Botany at the University of Cincinnati. The author came across an article written by The Olde Forester, Emmett A. Conway, Sr. that referenced a possible white oak Trail Marker Tree that he called a signal tree located in Lynx Prairie. A few years later, while the author was researching nearby effigy mounds, he brought the article by Conway and located the Trail Marker Tree. Unfortunately, the tree had fallen only days before; the

leaves were still on the tree's branches. The base of the fallen tree was nearly 130 inches in circumference, making the tree approximately 270 years old. The author believes this Trail Marker Tree would have led off the main trail towards Brush Creek. Adjacent to the fallen white oak Trail Marker Tree, there was another white oak in demise. The remains of this white oak, partially still standing, also appeared to have been a Trail Marker Tree.

Throughout this area, the Trail Marker Trees are often referred to as signal trees. Similarly, the nationally known Indian fire pits are known as signal bowls. The signal bowls or fire pits were used by the Native Americans as a way of communicating across long distances. Conway, The Olde Forester, has documented many possible signal bowls throughout Ohio. Weddington Hill is a site where some of these signal bowls are located; it is also said to have a Trail Marker Tree or signal tree. This possible Trail Marker Tree was discovered by a friend of Conway. Downes has not been able to visit the site of this possible Trail Marker Tree, but hopes to in the future. Although there are only a few documented Trail Marker Trees in the state of Ohio, the author hopes as more people become aware of these historical landmarks, more may be discovered. Some remote areas between the historical effigy mounds and ancient Indian sites are not as well traveled because of modern roads. Downes believes there may still be many undiscovered Trail Marker Trees amidst these less traveled remote areas.

This double trunk Trail Marker Tree stands in Woodville, Ohio and marks the shallow crossing point on the Portage River. Photo taken by Dale K. Benington.

A plaque designating Lynx Prairie as a National Landmark.

Dennis standing near the recently fallen Trail Marker Tree at Lynx Prairie.

PENNSYLVANIA

Pennsylvania was one of the original thirteen colonies and very important to the development of our country. At the arrival of the first Europeans, there were many Native American tribes in the area, including the Shawnee, the Iroquois, the Oneida, the Munsee, the Lenape, the Susquehannock, and the Erie. With the arrival of the early European settlers, many of the Native American tribes left the area as Pennsylvania become colonized.

Pennsylvania, named Penn's Woods after the respected William Penn, was covered in dense forests and known for its hilly and mountainous terrain. These hilly and mountainous areas were referred to by the Iroquois as "Tyannuntasacta," meaning endless hills. Due to the early colonization, many of the original Indian trails and pathways were quickly widened and expanded into well-known trails such as Braddock's Road (also known as Nemaolin's Path and the Cumberland Trail) and the Kittanning Trail. The early settlers began logging the forests quickly to supply the colonies with much needed timber for buildings and the profitable shipbuilding industry. Logging became a booming industry in the eastern colonies and continued even after the Revolutionary War. Oak was a prized timber for shipbuilders because of its strength and ability to hold natural curves and bends. The curved timbers used by shipbuilders to help strengthen the ships internally and build specific parts of the ships were called compass timbers. The shipbuilders would send out loggers specifically to find these valuable compass timbers along the many existing paths and trails through the forests. Unfortunately, many of the culturally modified Trail Marker Trees were harvested along with the naturally occurring bent and deformed trees.

Pennsylvania has few documented Trail Marker Trees, most likely due to its early colonization, logging, and early removal of the Native Americans to western lands. However, Pennsylvania is well-known for a different form of navigational marker, the Standing Stone. The Standing Stone was said to be at least 14 feet tall and six inches by six inches in width and depth; upon the stone there were ancient writings and symbols. In 1748, Conrad Weiser documented seeing the Standing Stone during one of his trips. Weiser was a pioneer, interpreter, judge, and worked for the provincial government. In his teens, Weiser lived among the Mohawk tribe to learn their language and practices. The Standing Stone was referred to by many other early explorers and settlers until it was removed in 1754. In 1896, a large memorial stone in the likeness of the original, was erected to commemorate the original Standing Stone. Upon the memorial stone was inscribed; "Onojutta Juniata Achsinnik Standing Stone erected Sept. 8th 1896, As a memorial of the ancient standing stone removed by the Indians in 1754."

The memorial stone can still be seen in Huntingdon today. Other sizeable upright stones were used as markers by the Native Americans on the east coast. Although these stones are not referenced as being as remarkable at the Huntingdon Standing Stone, most were at least six to seven feet tall and either round or square in shape. Some of these stones have been preserved and can be seen at the Stratford Connecticut Historical Society.

The prevalence of standing stones and other Neolithic stone works is far more common throughout Europe. The author has been to the United Kingdom on three occasions to research some of these well-known stone works and stone markers including the Ring of Brodgar, the Stones of Stenness,

page 205

This photograph appeared in the *Saturday Evening Post* in an article written by A. Franklin Wehr in 1948. This photograph was provided by Harold Kreger and Ruthanne Toner of Polk Township.

Dennis with Dr. Jane Downes, Head of Department and course team leader for Archaeology at Orkney College, and Timothy Downes, Geologist, near Tenby in southwest Wales.

The memorial of the original Standing Stone of Huntingdon; this memorial is still standing today.

This is a photograph of a stitching made for Harold Kreger by a friend commemorating the Trail Marker Tree that stood on their family farm. This photograph was provided by Ben Kreger.

Stonehenge, and Avebury. The author was able to spend over a month with respected archeologists and other experts during his research at these archeological sites. During one of his trips, Dennis was able to present his educational Trail Marker Tree Exhibit at the Pier Arts Centre in Stromness, Orkney. This exhibit included Downes' first bronze "Trail Marker Tree" sculpture. The author's research of standing stones in the United Kingdom broadened his perspective when his research of North American navigational markers brought him to the use of standing stones in our eastern states.

In the early 1940s, Dr. Raymond Janssen documented two Trail Marker Trees near Kresgeville, Pennsylvania. One of these trees was an elm and the other was a white oak. Unfortunately, the elm was blown down by strong winds shortly after it was documented at over 200 years old. However, the white oak continued to stand for many decades into the 1960s. This white oak Trail Marker Tree was a double trunk and stood on the Kreger's farm for generations. The author discovered an article written in the 1940s about these trees and tried locating more information about them for years. Finally, with the help of Ruthanne Toner of Polk Township, Downes was able to find more information. Ruthanne was able to put Downes in touch with Harold Kreger, a third-generation Kreger still living on the family farm. Mr. Kreger and his son, Ben Kreger, spoke with the author and provided photographs and written documentation about the Trail Marker Tree that

The author during his research at the Ring of Brodgar in 1999. Photograph taken by archeologist, Jane Downes.

This photograph was taken by the author during his research at Avebury.

This photograph of the double trunk Trail Marker Tree that stood on the Kreger Farm appeared in a local newspaper in the 1940's. Pictured in front of the Trail Marker Tree are E.C. Pyle, the Delaware District Forester, and Dr. Nathan G. Meyer, the recording secretary of the Monroe County Historical Society. This photograph was provided by Harold Kreger and Ruthanne Toner of Polk Township.

stood on his family farm. The double trunk Trail Marker Tree was included in *Polk Township's Historical Book* written in 1996. Dr. Frank Grover also documented Trail Marker Trees near the Braddock Trail, east of Allegheny City, in the early 1900s. The author's continued contact with the Pennsylvania area has generated an increased interest and awareness about the Trail Marker Trees. The author is grateful to both Ruthanne Toner and the Kreger Family for their help with this project.

Chapter Eleven

NEW YORK

New York State was inhabited by Native Americans for thousands of years. The Six Nations, also known as the Iroquois Confederacy, was formed as early as 1090 and included the Oneidas, Onondagas, Mohawks, Senecas, Cayugas, and later the Tuscaroras. The Iroquois Confederacy is documented as being the earliest participatory democracy. The breathtaking New York landscape includes numerous mountain ranges such as the Appalachians, Catskills, and Adirondacks, as well as the beautiful Finger Lakes Region, and is bordered by both the Great Lakes and the Atlantic Ocean. There were numerous Native American trails and pathways that helped the Native Americans navigate the sometimes treacherous landscape.

One of the most famous trails, the Mohawk Trail, also known as the Iroquois Trail, led from Albany City to Buffalo connecting the Atlantic Ocean to the Great Lakes.

However, as one of the earliest colonized states, New York's Native American past was soon replaced by the European way of life. In 1609, Henry Hudson claimed New York for the Dutch and by 1664, the British had taken over the land. The pathways and trails were quickly turned into roads, railroads, and eventually highways. In his book, *The Almond Story* published in 1962, John Reynolds states: "*These trails avoided natural obstructions and followed the contour of this land so well that many of our present highways follow their courses... alongside a road that branches off Karr Valley toward what is known as Bully Hill, is an Indian trail-marker tree which is identified by a sign and is reputed to be 250 years old. This tree exemplifies a means the Indians used to mark their trails for direction or other purposes.*" New York's early colonization, shipbuilding industry, and rapid population growth all would have contributed to the quick demise of the Trail Marker Trees. The Trail Marker Trees along the established paths and trails would be the first to be removed for shipbuilding, again because of the easy accessibility.

Downes has traveled extensively throughout New York, focusing his research along many of the old Indian pathways such as the Iroquois Trail, which today is followed closely by State Route 90. The author also visited local historical societies, arboretums, and nature centers throughout the state. During his research, Downes became familiar with the well-known "lopped trees" of Long Island. While these "lopped trees" are not Native American Trail Marker Trees, they are known as cultural landmarks. They were formed on property lines and used as references in early land surveys. The "lopped trees" and similarly shaped plashed trees were used to fence in properties and to keep in cows and sheep. In 1790, George Washington commented on these fencing methods in his diary, writing; "*Their fences, where there is no stone, are very indifferent: frequently of plashed trees of any and every kind which have grown by chance.*" Washington further went on to state that this method of fencing, which would have been similar to hedge laying found in Britain, was not "Hog Tight." The remains of some of these "lopped" and plashed trees can be seen throughout New York.

In some cases, trees may bear resemblance to the Native American Trail Marker Trees, but they were modified by the Europeans for different purposes. Similarly, 'line trees' and 'witness trees' were modified by surveyors and landowners to denote survey and property lines. They have also been confused with Trail Marker Trees on many occasions. In the past, trees were shaped and modified out of necessity. However, today, modifying and shaping trees has become an art form. Arborsculpture, as it has been termed, is becoming very popular across the United States.

page 211
This photograph shows two Trail Marker Trees in close proximity at the Jersey Hill State Forest. This photograph was provided by Lee and Donna Ryan of the Almond Historical Society, New York.

This double trunk Trail Marker Tree located in Michigan along a highway that was once an Indian trail bears a striking resemblance both in age and shape to the double trunk Trail Marker Tree located near Bully Hill, New York. Photo taken by Patrick John Downes.

This photograph by Josienita Borlongan, shows a modern example of tree modification termed Arborsculpture. Arborsculpture can be seen at parks and gardens across the country. This particular Arborsculpture was created by Axel Erlandson.

following page
This photo was taken in 1960 and was accompanied by the note: "M. Earl Dungan and the Indian Trail Tree on the Bully Hill Road that goes from Karr Valley Road up into Bully Hill. Taken by a photographer for the Alfred Sun on Monday, July 18, 1960. Eugene VanHorn, editor of the Alfred Sun was with us too." This photograph was provided by Lee and Donna Ryan of the Almond Historical Society, New York.

Lee and Donna Ryan of the Almond Historical Society have been researching and documenting Trail Marker Trees in the state of New York for approximately a decade. The Ryan's were charter members of the Almond Historical Society in 1965 and have had several articles about the Trail Marker Trees published in the Historical Society Newsletter; they also had an article, *Indian Trail Trees* published in *Whispering Wind*, a bi-monthly Native American magazine. The efforts put forth by the Ryan's and other local historians have created a greater awareness and interest in the Trail Marker Trees throughout their area and the greater state of New York. The Ryan's have been in contact with Downes for a number of years, exchanging photographs and articles regarding Trail Marker Trees. The author was able to provide some valuable information and guidance to aid the Ryan's in their research. After many conversations and written correspondence with Downes, the Ryan's thanked him for his assistance and stated, "...*Again, we are sorry we did not get acquainted much earlier. We would have been better researchers, I am sure...had we been tutored by you and your valuable knowledge.*" The Ryan's have continued their enthusiasm and research of the Trail Marker Trees, and the author plans to visit them in New York to personally view some of the trees they have located. The author hopes that through the efforts of individuals such as the Ryan's, more Trail Marker Trees will be located throughout the magnificent forests of the New England states.

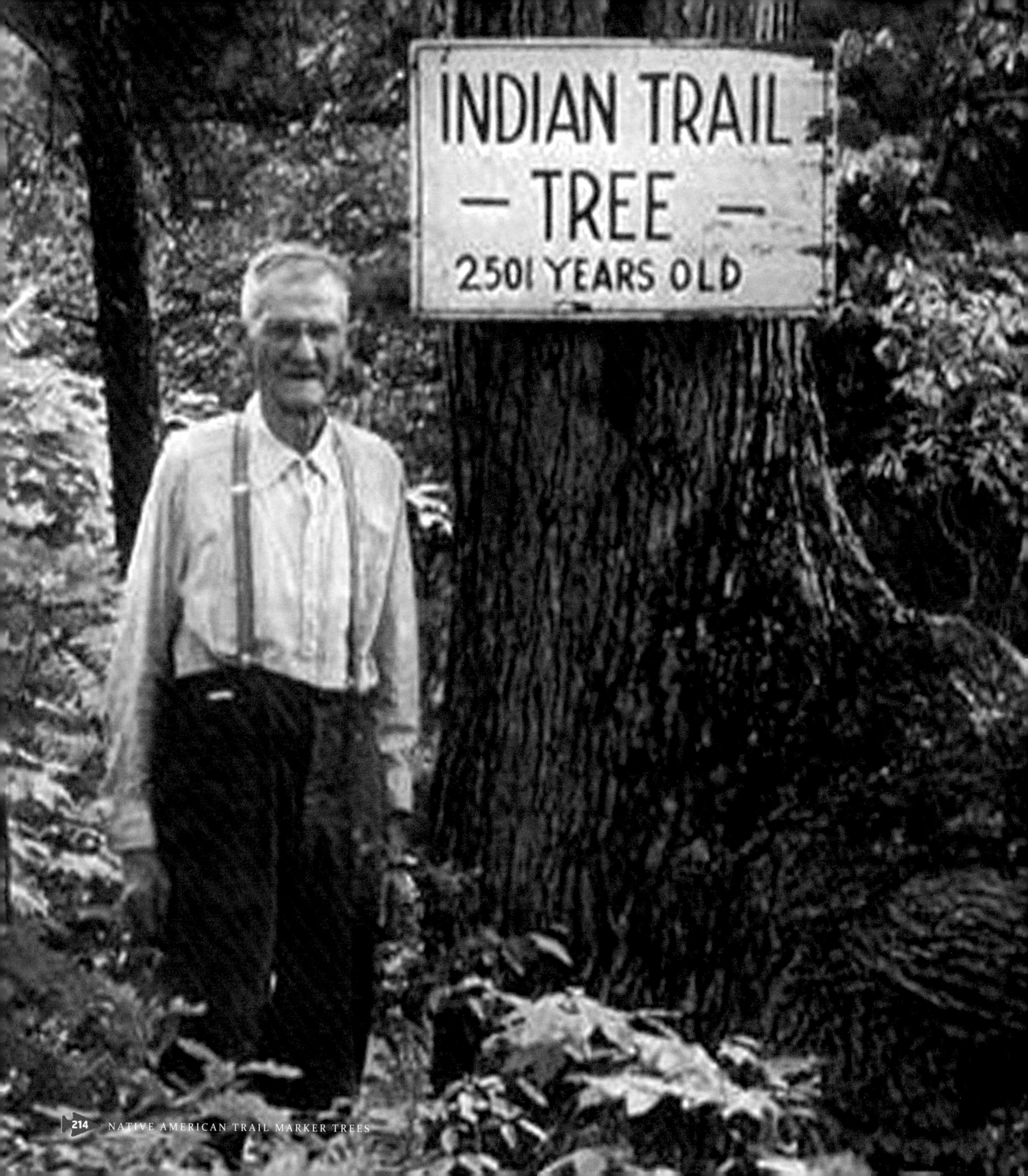
INDIAN TRAIL
— TREE —
2501 YEARS OLD

 *Chapter Twelve*

SOUTHEASTERN STATES

The southeastern United States also has a beautiful and varied geography; much of the region is bordered by the Atlantic Ocean. Although no official definition exists, it is generally accepted that the southeastern region is comprised of Alabama, Arkansas, Florida, Georgia, Kentucky, Louisiana, Mississippi, North Carolina, South Carolina, Tennessee, Virginia, and West Virginia.

Parts of this southeastern region are crossed by the Appalachian and Blue Ridge Mountains, full of beauty and majesty. Spectacular waterfalls, lakes, and rivers, as well as dense forests can also be found throughout the region. The southeast has a strong connection to its Native American history and the many tribes that once occupied the area. Some of the American Indian tribes from the southeast are the Cherokee, Natchez, Tuscarora, Creek, Choctaw, Seminole, Chicasaw, and many others. There are over 100 documented Indian trails crisscrossing the southeastern states. Some of these paths and trails were trade routes that would connect the Gulf Coast to the Great Lakes Region.

These trade routes are supported by archeological findings such as shells and copper adornments from the south dating back to 6000 B.C., located in Great Lakes Region mounds. In 1925, William Myer and John Swanton documented scores of pathways and trails in *Indian Trails of the Southeast,* an excerpt from the *42nd Annual Report of the Bureau of American Ethnology*. One of the most important trails was the Great Indian Warpath. This system of pathways was used in both times of war and times of peace for trading and travel. The Great Indian Warpath stretched from New York, near the Niagara Falls, through Pennsylvania, to the Shenandoah Valley to the Tennessee River, and onto the Chattanooga area in Georgia and Alabama. Branches off of the Great Indian Warpath connected areas in Mississippi, the Cumberland Gap into Kentucky, and even the Carolinas. Many of the modern roads

and highways in the southeast follow parts of this old extensive trail system including U.S. Highway 11. Hernando de Soto traveled along parts of the Great Indian Warpath during his 1540 expedition. Another well-known ancient trail is the Old Chicasaw Trace, which connected modern-day Nashville near the Big Salt Lick, onto Pontotoc, Mississippi. However, there were more than 100 documented trails and pathways that helped the early Native American to navigate the southeast's mountains, river crossings, swamps, bayous, and dense forests. It is no doubt that the Trail Marker Trees would have been great navigational aids throughout this area of the country as well. Numerous Trail Marker Trees have been documented in the southeastern states as a result of early efforts to preserve these historical landmarks by Native Americans, early pioneers, and settlers.

The author has been traveling through and visiting the southeastern states since the 1960s. By the 1980s, Downes had spent months at a time in the southeastern states researching Trail Marker Trees, rock outcroppings and caves, natural springs, and the river systems. In 1997, Downes participated in the Tennessee River Cruise hosted by the Dixieland Chapter of the Antique and Classic Boat Society, navigating 400 miles from Guntersville, Alabama to Clarksville, Kentucky by boat. The author has continued to travel to the southeastern states for research up to the present day. During his many trips, Downes has worked with foresters, historians, nature centers, and arboretums to gain further information about the area

page 217
Michael Steinback, a friend of the author, had attended Trail Marker Tree lectures and exhibits in the past and informed Dennis of a double trunk Trail Marker Tree located near his family's home in Ashville, North Carolina. Dennis stopped to visit the Steinback's during a research trip through the southeast. The Steinback's children, Matt and Megan, took Dennis to see the Trail Marker Tree so he could photograph it and take measurements. Megan is seen here sitting on the tree as a young girl. Photograph taken by the author.

Downes in his 1939 wooden boat, The Phantom Chief, on the Tennessee River. James Staib, President of the Black Hawk Chapter of the Antique and Classic Boat Society from Illinois, and Jude Kitts accompanied the author on this 400 mile trip.

Dennis joined by his lifelong friends, Gary Rusch and vocalist Peter Quinn, on the author's 1939

classic wooden boat that was restored in the Channel Lakes Region, Illinois. The Phantom Chief was restored over a ten year period through the efforts of many members of the Black Hawk Chapter of the Antique and Classic Boat Society. Photo taken by Gail Spreen.

The author's nephew, Patrick Downes, standing by this traditional Trail Marker Tree growing on rugged terrain. This oak Trail Marker Tree stands in Monterey, Tennessee; this town is known for the legendary standing stone that was said to mark the territory between the Shawnee and Cherokee lands. The town of Monterey was originally named Standing Stone. Traditional Native American ceremonies are still held to honor the standing stone in Monterey today; a remnant of the original twelve foot standing stone still remains as a monument in the town. Photo taken by the author.

and possible Trail Marker Trees. Throughout the years, Downes has presented educational exhibits and provided informational pamphlets to many locations in the southeast during his research trips that have helped to generate awareness and interest in the Trail Marker Trees.

During the mid-1990s there was a pronounced increase in interest regarding the Trail Marker Trees in the southeast. In 1995, the author was contacted by Elaine Jordan regarding her interest in the Trail Marker Trees throughout the Georgia area. Jordan was born in Wisconsin and later worked as a journalist for the *Herald News* in Joliet, Illinois. Jordan had contacted many Illinois historical societies to obtain information regarding the Trail Marker Trees and one of the historical societies referred Jordan to the author; Jordan had visited Downes' educational website before contacting him. Downes had several conversations over the following year with Jordan and referred her to several historians as well as old articles that had been written in the past. The following year, Jordan published a short paperback about the Trail Marker Trees in her area. The book generated a great deal of interest in the Trail Marker Trees throughout the southeast. Unfortunately, it also provoked some controversy. Jordan's paperback used multiple names for the Trail Marker Trees, such as thong trees, language trees, horse and rider trees, and message trees. Some of the examples portrayed in the book also generated controversy over their authenticity. Jordan did include several good examples of Trail Marker Trees, however,

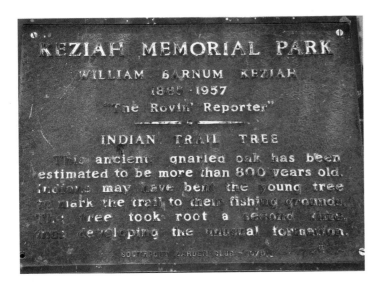

KEZIAH MEMORIAL PARK
WILLIAM BARNUM KEZIAH
1885 - 1957
"The Rovin' Reporter"

INDIAN TRAIL TREE
This ancient gnarled oak has been
estimated to be more than 800 years old.
Indians may have bent the young tree
to mark the trail to their fishing grounds.
The tree took root a second time,
thus developing the unusual formation.
SOUTHPORT GARDEN CLUB - 1979

many of which were located in Georgia.

Later, in 2007, the author was contacted by a group called the Mountain Stewards. This group originated in Georgia with the initial goal to preserve and restore hiking trails and paths throughout the Southern Appalachian area. Through their efforts to preserve and restore hiking trails, they became aware of the Trail Marker Trees. The President of the Mountain Stewards, Don Wells, contacted Downes to gain his advice and council to aid the Mountain Stewards in their project. In a correspondence to the author Mr. Wells wrote:

"The Mountain Stewards has been studying and documenting Indian Trail Trees in North GA for about five years, way short of what you have accomplished in the Great Lakes Region and elsewhere. We located your web site and were very impressed with what you have accomplished in the past few decades documenting the legacy of the Indian Trail Trees."

The Mountain Stewards hoped to make a documentary about the Trail Marker Trees and Downes believed this could be a beneficial project. He informed Mr. Wells about the documentary created by the Northbrook Arts Commission in 2003 based on his study of the Trail Marker Trees; it aired on the Illinois cable channels. The author also expressed to Mr. Wells his belief in preserving the credibility and integrity of the study. Referring to non-authentic examples of young or simply deformed trees as Trail Marker Trees could cause confusion and doubt. One of the main concerns the author had in regards to the Mountain

This plaque commemorates the ancient Trail Marker Tree in Keziah Memorial Park, North Carolina. It is inscribed: "Indian Trail Tree: This ancient, gnarled oak has been estimated to be more than 800 years old. Indians may have bent the young tree to mark the trail to their fishing grounds. The tree took root a second time, thus developing the unusual formation. Southport Garden Club–1975" This photo was courteously provided by J. J. Prats, Editor and Publisher of the Historical Marker Database.

This ancient oak is said to be one of the oldest living Trail Marker Trees in the south, located in North Carolina. A photograph of this tree was used for a postcard nearly 100 years ago, where the bent portion of the tree can still be seen clearly above ground. Today, this Trail Marker Tree is protected and denoted by a plaque placed by the Southport Garden Club. This photo was courteously provided by J. J. Prats, Editor and Publisher of the Historical Marker Database.

Since the author's trip in the 1990's, the neighborhood was made aware of the historical significance of this Trail Marker Tree and has made conscientious efforts to preserve and protect this tree. Years later a home was built on the same lot the Trail Marker Tree was located on and the landscapers and contractors ensured the tree was spared. This photograph shows Megan sitting in the same tree in May of 2011. This photograph was courteously provided by the Steinback Family.

This double trunk Trail Marker Tree is located near Greensville, South Carolina; this old oak has a diameter of over three feet. Tony Weaks located this Trail Marker Tree and has been working with Downes trying to locate other examples in his area. Upon researching the area, Mr. Weaks spoke with a local farmer who confirmed that a fresh water spring was located near the Trail Marker Tree. Photo provided by Tony Weaks.

This traditional Trail Marker Tree is located in Gilmer County Georgia, in the foothills of the Appalachian Mountains. Brian and Nadine Buchholz are pictured with the author in this photograph. Photo taken by Gail Spreen.

Stewards was their plan to provide GPS coordinates to every documented Trail Marker Tree on public and private properties. Downes strongly believes that the Trail Marker Trees should be protected just as endangered species, since there are very few authentic culturally modified Trail Marker Trees remaining. In his efforts to ensure these trees are protected, Downes engaged the services of attorney Terrence R. Lyons Jr., also a historian and Trail Marker Tree advocate, to contact state officials regarding the importance of protecting these historical landmarks. Based on the author's past experience, he has seen numerous Trail Marker Trees become damaged when their exact locations were released. Downes believes in protecting these historical landmarks and only including trees in the study that are old enough to have been shaped by the Native Americans and portray certain characteristics that could not have been caused by nature alone.

Throughout the southeast there are numerous examples of past and present Trail Marker Trees. Through the combined efforts of historians, garden clubs, Trail Marker Tree advocates, and others, many traditional Trail Marker Trees have continued to be documented and protected.

This ancient Trail Marker Tree is located near Atlanta on property that was sold to the Georgia State University in 1938 to be used as a retreat and recreation area for the faculty and staff, located off campus. Luckily, this property has remained under the control of the University and has not been developed, preserving this historical Trail Marker Tree. Pictured here taking measurements of this tree is John Krafka, the Associate Director of the Department of Recreational Services for the Georgia State University. This traditional Trail Marker Tree has a circumference of fourteen feet at the base and twelve feet at the bend. John courteously submitted this photo and many others as well as some historical information about this Trail Marker Tree to the author.

This photograph, taken by John Krafka, pictures this excellent example of an Native American Trail Marker Tree in Georgia. John located a fresh water spring approximately fifty yards from the tree and believes the Trail Marker Tree would have been leading to this fresh water source. John has been protecting and caring for this ancient landmark out of respect for its historical and Native American significance.

This photograph of a double trunk Trail Marker Tree was taken in Georgia, not far from the Chattahoochee National Forest. This photograph was taken and submitted by John Stutz.

Downes standing behind a Chinquapin Oak Boundary Tree located in the William Bankhead National Forest, Alabama. Downes was joined on this research trip by Brian and Nadine Buchholz. This well-known Marker Tree stands upon a geographical divide. Two Trail Marker Tree advocates that have researched many trails and Trail Marker Trees throughout the Alabama area are Lamar Marshall the Cultural Heritage Director of Wild South and Rickey Butch Walker author and Director of the Indian Education Program for Lawrence County Schools.

Chapter Thirteen

ARKANSAS

Today, much of Arkansas' landscape is still as it would have appeared to the ancient Native Americans and the first settlers many years ago. The appeal and natural resources of this area drew the Native Americans as far back as 9500 B.C. Arkansas boasts over half a million acres of major and minor lakes with over 9,000 miles of rivers and streams. Arkansas also offers a mild climate, numerous rock shelters and caves, fertile land along the Mississippi, and the famed hot springs.

This region would have provided a wealth of hunting and fishing for the Native Americans along with fertile lands for cultivation and areas of shelter. In the early 1800s some of the Native American tribes that were said to be occupying the area were the Quapaw, Osage, Choctaw, Caddo, and Cherokee. Throughout Arkansas, remnants of the Native Americans can still be seen today, including numerous Trail Marker Trees, preserved sections of famous Indian trails, and remains of ancient Indian occupation sites. Many of the modern highways throughout the state of Arkansas follow routes of the old Indian trails. Arkansas Highway 265 follows the path of the Great Osage Trail; it was first turned into a stage coach line and eventually a highway. The historic Trail of Tears runs through the state of Arkansas. It was not one single path but rather several paths and trails utilized to forcibly remove the Cherokee people from their homelands and relocate them to Oklahoma. Today, over 2,000 miles of trails have been documented as part of the Trail of Tears.

Ruth and Robert, a couple living in Arkansas, contacted the author regarding several possible Trail Marker Trees they believed to be located on their property in White County, as well as possible Native American ovens. Downes and the couple corresponded through email and phone conversations until he was able to make a trip to their area of the state. During the research trip, the couple showed Downes a number of possible Trail Marker Trees and the Indian ovens they had previously told him about. Ruth, now in her 60s, explained

previous page
One of the Trail Marker Trees along the route Ruth and Robert took Dennis to get to the interesting archeological site. Photo taken by the author.

Ruth and Robert leading the way on their property in Arkansas. Photo taken by the author

Dennis in a rock shelter near the Indian ovens Ruth's relatives first taught her about when she was seven years old. Photo taken by Ruth.

Ruth standing next to one of the Indian ovens that had been carved into the rock face. Photo taken by the author.

A similarly shaped Indian oven also in good condition with limited deterioration. These Indian ovens are located along the creek bed and are all approximately the same dimensions. Photo taken by the author.

A fourth Indian oven also located at the same site, also in demise. Photo taken by the author.

page 228–229
A close up of a third Indian oven showing greater deterioration. Photo taken by the author.

how the knowledge of the Indian ovens had been passed down to her as a little girl from her older family relatives going back three generations. While on Ruth and Robert's property, the author located two possible Trail Marker Trees. Robert also showed Downes a year-round freshwater spring that was located near one of the Trail Marker Tree sites. The combination of the Trail Marker Trees, Indian ovens built into the rock face, and the nearby fresh water spring makes this site a true archeological treasure. The preserved condition of this site makes it possible to visualize the Native Americans still living there and using the stone ovens and fresh water spring. The author encouraged the couple to have their rare and interesting site visited and documented by local archeologists and Native American experts.

Near the same time, the author was again contacted in regards to a different Trail Marker Tree in Arkansas. Susan Rush, niece of a Hobbs State Park employee, sent Downes a photo of her favorite Trail Marker Tree that she had been calling the "deer tree" because of its odd shape and resemblance to a deer. Susan actually lives in Illinois, but saw this tree while visiting her uncle over Thanksgiving. Susan's uncle, Steve Chyrchel, has known about the Trail Marker Trees in Hobbs State Park for quite a while and took his niece to see three Trail Marker Trees during her visit. Steve Chyrchel is a Certified Interpretive Guide and the park interpreter for Hobbs State Park Conservation Area. The author was able to contact Chyrchel to plan a research trip to the park to see the trees that Chyrchel had located. Before Downes traveled to Arkansas,

he contacted the Arkansas State Historical Society, which referred him to A.D. Poole, the past president of the Washington County Historical Society and board member of the Heritage Trail Partners, Inc. Poole's family had resided in Arkansas since the 1850's and he was able to provide the author with further historical information about the area. Poole also recommended that Downes contact Glenn Jones, a Native American from the area. Jones is the Vice President and National Board Representative of the Arkansas Chapter Trail of Tears Association; he also is the commissioner of the Benton County Historical Preservation Commission. Jones spoke with Downes about the occurrence of Trail Marker Trees in areas of known Native American occupation. They also discussed that it was unlikely that any Trail Marker Trees would have been shaped along the Trail of Tears. Some groups have proposed that the Native Americans shaped numerous Trail Marker Trees along the Trail of Tears during their forced exile. However, Downes and Jones do not believe that the Native Americans would have had the freedom or time to complete the shaping of a Trail Marker Tree during a forced march. They agreed, however, that this does not mean Trail Marker Trees were not already in existence along this route before the march. Downes planned to include a meeting with Jones during his next visit to the Arkansas area.

When Downes traveled to Arkansas, he first met with Glenn Jones and Bill Carter, a Native American, in Benton County. Carter and Jones took Downes to see a Trail

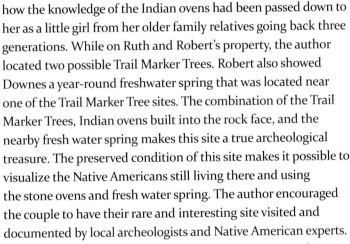

Marker Tree near Carter's home. Jones and Carter took Downes to several important historical and heritage sites throughout the Benton and Washington County area. Jones also took the author to the Crystal Bridges project. Today the building is completed and is the Museum of American Art, honoring America's heritage. The author discussed his plan to visit Hobbs State Park with Jones and Carter. Jones thought this would be a successful visit since he believed the Hobbs State Park to be the old Osage hunting grounds.

During the visit to Hobbs State Park, Downes was able to meet with Steve Chyrchel and other park officials. He gave a short presentation about his Trail Marker Tree study and they recommended that he make a return trip later in the year to also meet with Al Knox, the trail maintenance supervisor for the Department of Parks and Tourism. Downes and his wife, Gail, hiked through and researched Hobbs State Park and were able to locate some of the existing Trail Marker Trees.

Later that year, the author was able to make a return trip to Hobbs State Park and meet with Al Knox. Knox had taken a great interest in the Trail Marker Trees and had been working to educate the public in the area about these historical landmarks. Downes met with Steve Chyrchel and other park officials to discuss the Trail Marker Tree study in greater detail. After the meeting, Downes and Knox hiked to locate numerous Trail Marker Trees throughout the park. The staff at Hobbs State Park is continuing to try and educate the public about these historically significant Trail Marker Trees

previous page left
The year round fresh water source located near the site of the Indian ovens. Photo taken by the author.

previous page right
This photograph was sent to Dennis by Susan Rush of Illinois. She photographed this Trail Marker Tree when visiting her Uncle, Steve Chyrchel a Certified Interpretive Guide of the Department of Parks and Tourism. This is Susan's favorite Trail Marker Tree in the park and she believes it bears a strong resemblance to a deer head. Photo taken by Susan Rush.

Dennis was shown this Trail Marker Tree by Glenn Jones.

Dennis with Glenn Jones and Bill Carter. During this trip Jones and Bill Carter took Dennis to see a fresh water spring near the Trail Marker Tree and numerous historical and heritage sites.

One of the first Trail Marker Trees Dennis located on his trip to Hobbs State Park; this double trunk Trail Marker Tree is located near the Shaddox Hollow Trailhead. This photo was taken the first night Dennis and his wife arrived in Arkansas during this trip. Previously, Glenn Jones had told the author about the location of this Trail Marker Tree. Photo taken by Gail Spreen.

page 235–235
This photograph overlooking Beaver Lake was taken by the author on the morning following his arrival to the Hobbs State Park area on his way back to the park showing the beautiful landscape and scenery in the area.

as well as the important trails they would have helped to navigate. Downes has continued to work with Glenn Jones to locate more Trail Marker Trees throughout the state. Jones hopes to have one of Downes' bronze Trail Marker Tree sculptures placed in a historically significant location to commemorate this form of land navigation used by the Native Americans. The author is grateful and appreciative for the acceptance and reception of his work and Trail Marker Tree study by the Native American community and other Trail Marker Tree advocates in Arkansas.

"*I met Dennis Downes while he was researching Trail Marker Trees in my area of Arkansas. Since that time I have come to admire Mr. Downes' research and artwork. I and many others would love to have one of Mr. Downes' bronze Trail Marker Tree sculptures on prominent display at an appropriate site in our area.*" Glenn Jones, vice president and National Board Representative of the Arkansas Chapter Trail of Tears Association; Commissioner of the Benton County Historical Preservation Commission

Dennis at the entrance to Hobbs State Park. Photo taken by Gail Spreen.

Dennis revisited this Trail Marker Tree the following morning in the daylight to get a better look, his wife Gail is pictured by the tree. Photo taken by the author.

Downes and Al Knox next to the same Trail Marker Tree that Susan Rush had previously emailed Downes about. This specific shape of Trail Marker Tree occurs in a number of states and varies slightly from the more traditional Trail Marker Tree shape.

This Trail Marker Tree located in Illinois has a strong resemblance to the Trail Marker Tree located in Hobbs State Park. This tree was photographed over 100 years ago and has changed very little in size and shape since that time. It was documented by Dr. Raymond Janssen in the 1930's and was marking an intersection of two trails.

Al Knox, the Trail Maintenance Supervisor for the Department of Parks and Tourism, took the author to see this classic example of a Trail Marker Tree in the Hobbs State Park.

Dennis with Al Knox looking at another example of a traditional Trail Marker Tree located in Hobbs State Park.

Chapter Fourteen

TEXAS

The sheer size of Texas makes it a notably impressive state. When combined with its diverse and beautiful landscape, it is truly remarkable. The Lone Star State is larger than a number of countries around the world; Texas has over 260,000 square miles, making its square mileage more than five times that of New York's total square mileage. Parts of Texas are covered in mountainous terrain. In western Texas, Guadalupe Peak, part of the Guadalupe Mountains, is the highest point in the state at 8,751 feet high.

Texas also has thousands of miles of rivers and streams that run through the state, including the Rio Grande that runs along the southern border of Texas. Although there are many naturally formed rivers, Texas has very few naturally formed lakes. During the twentieth century, the Army Corps of Engineers constructed numerous manmade lakes across the state to help control flooding and to benefit the agricultural industry. The many different geographical regions throughout the state range from forested rolling hills, prairies, and desert grasslands to desert valleys, steep mountains, and dense hardwood forests. The state also has been classified with 10 distinct climactic regions. The ancient people of this state were as diverse as its landscape and climate, each adjusting to their own varied regions. Some of the Native American tribes that occupied the area when the first Europeans arrived were the Comanche, Apache (Lipan), Caddo, Tonkawa, Coahuiltecan, Karankawa, Cherokee, Kiowa, and Hasinai. The word "Texas" was said to originate from the Hasinai word for friend.

During ancient times, the varied geographic and climactic regions in Texas in combination with the limited access to fresh water springs and lakes would have made accurate navigation very imperative to the Native American way of life. Throughout the state, many different forms of navigational aids were used by the Native Americans, such as Trail Marker Trees, petroglyphs, pictographs, and stone markers. In Texas, many of the old Indian trails and pathways would later be used by the cattle drovers and eventually be turned into modern roads

previous page
This photo of the Texas wilderness was taken by the author during a trip near Squaw Mountain.

Dennis' family has had long ties with the Boy Scouts of America; here his oldest brother Lou (center) is pictured wearing his Boy Scout uniform before leaving for a jamboree. Also pictured are Dennis' older brother Harry (left), his younger brother Patrick (center), and Dennis (right).

Dennis also participated in Cub Scouts for a number of years as a young boy and so did his brother Patrick, his mother served as a Den Leader; here is mother Mary (left), Dennis (center), his brother Patrick (right).

Dennis' nephew, Matt, standing behind the pecan Trail Marker Tree that he and his father, Patrick, photographed and took measurements of for Dennis. This triple trunk Trail Marker Tree closely resembles the triple trunk Trail Marker Tree that was located in the Evanston, Illinois area. Both triple trunk trees were said to signify the location of an Indian Village.

Dennis' nephew, Matt, after receiving his ranking as an Eagle Scout, the highest rank attainable in the Boy Scouts of America.

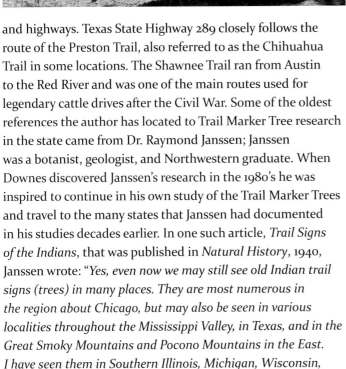

and highways. Texas State Highway 289 closely follows the route of the Preston Trail, also referred to as the Chihuahua Trail in some locations. The Shawnee Trail ran from Austin to the Red River and was one of the main routes used for legendary cattle drives after the Civil War. Some of the oldest references the author has located to Trail Marker Tree research in the state came from Dr. Raymond Janssen; Janssen was a botanist, geologist, and Northwestern graduate. When Downes discovered Janssen's research in the 1980's he was inspired to continue in his own study of the Trail Marker Trees and travel to the many states that Janssen had documented in his studies decades earlier. In one such article, *Trail Signs of the Indians*, that was published in *Natural History*, 1940, Janssen wrote: *"Yes, even now we may still see old Indian trail signs (trees) in many places. They are most numerous in the region about Chicago, but may also be seen in various localities throughout the Mississippi Valley, in Texas, and in the Great Smoky Mountains and Pocono Mountains in the East. I have seen them in Southern Illinois, Michigan, Wisconsin, Ohio, Indiana, Kentucky, Tennessee, Missouri and Arkansas."*

Downes has been able to spend a great deal of time in Texas for both research and visits to family. Dennis' father, Harold Matthew Downes, is buried at the Dallas-Fort Worth National Cemetery; he served in the Air Corps during World War II. Dennis' brother, Patrick Downes, his wife Kim, and their three children, Kelly, Josh, and Matt also live in Texas.

Downes has been visiting his brother and family yearly since the 1980s; each year they embark on hunting, fishing, and hiking trips in the wilderness areas of the state. Patrick Downes has participated as a committee chairman and Merit Badge Counselor for the Boy Scouts of America, representing Troop 1134 Circle Ten Council in Plano, Texas, for the past 18 years. Patrick's oldest son, Josh, has earned the rank of Life Scout, and Matt has earned the rank of Eagle Scout. Downes has been able to share his knowledge of the Trail Marker Trees with his brother and nephews and they in turn have been able to educate other Boy Scouts about these historical landmarks. Patrick has also taught fellow Scout Leaders and business associates about the Trail Marker Trees.

Patrick and his son Matthew located a pecan Trail Marker Tree during a trip to Holliday, Texas. The tree was a triple trunk tree that appeared to be pointing to a large creek located nearby. After more research, Patrick and Matt came across an article, written by Ken Fibbe, that discussed the Trail Marker Tree they had located and a very similarly shaped Trail Marker Tree located in Florissant, Colorado that they had previously seen photos of from Dennis. Years earlier, the author had visited the petrified forests in the Florissant area on several occasions and documented the triple trunk Trail Maker Tree that was discussed in the article. Don Briix, a retired school principal, was riding his bike in Holliday when he recognized the triple trunk pecan tree as a Trail Marker Tree. In the article, Briix said, *"I remember saying, 'Oh my goodness,*

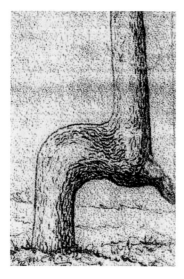

I think that is an Indian Marker Tree!'" Briix first saw a Trail Marker Tree in Florissant and has been knowledgeable and fascinated about them ever since. Linda Pelon and Steve Houser were also interviewed in this article. After reading the article, Downes was able to contact both Pelon and Houser.

Pelon is a cultural anthropologist and is currently an anthropology and history instructor at McLennan Community College. Much of her work has focused on the Texas Comanche ethnohistory and the preservation of cultural heritage sites. In 1997, she was proclaimed the Honorary Ambassador for the Comanche Nation. Steve Houser has been an arborist for over 30 years. He is a Master Gardener and the founding member of the Dallas Historic Tree Coalition. He teaches the North Texas Chapter of the Texas Master Naturalists, as well as other local chapters, and regional Master Gardener chapters each year about tree and forest-related subjects. He offers public presentations through both groups as well as the City of Dallas Urban Forest Advisory Committee, which he founded and chaired for four years. For over 15 years, both Pelon and Houser have helped to locate, protect, and honor Trail Marker Trees in Texas. Over the years, Dr. Richard Francaviglia has served as a valuable resource to both Pelon and Houser in their studies; Dr. Francaviglia is a Professor Emeritus of History and Geography. Several major groups including the Master Gardeners, Citizen Foresters, Master Naturalists, and the Texas Parks and Wildlife have contributed to the preservation efforts led by Pelon and Houser.

During the author's correspondence with Pelon and Houser, he was able to obtain numerous historical and recent references to the Trail Marker Trees in the state of Texas. In 1941, an article was published by the Dallas Archeological Society about a line of Trail Marker Trees located in Dallas County near Irving. All five trees were post oaks, from the white oak family. The publication also included sketches of the Trail Marker Trees that were located in Dallas County. This article was written as a result of the ongoing research conducted by Dr. Raymond Janssen and his articles that were published in the *Natural History, Scientific Monthly,* and *Nature Magazine.* In 1984, the Texas Forest Service wrote, *"The Comanches had several trails. At the better camping sites along a trail, a sapling-size tree was bent to the ground and tied down to serve as a marker. As the tree grew, it maintained this prostrate or horizontal position...a living monument to the presence of these early residents of Central Texas."* In 1996, Linda Pelon included this quote in her nomination of the Trail Marker Tree located in the Gateway Park, Lower White Rock Creek, to become a Dallas Historic Tree. In 1997, Wallace E. Coffey, chairman of the Comanche Indian Tribe, officially proclaimed the Trail Marker Tree in Gateway Park to be a historic Indian Marker Tree. On the official Comanche Proclamation, Coffey wrote: *"...through Comanche oral tradition it was common practice for our ancestors to tie a tree to the ground to serve as a marker and to give direction toward safety and security from our enemies...the Comanche Indian Tribe believes it is appropriate*

Steve Houser, Certified Arborist, pictured with Mayor Laura Miller during the "Mayor's Challenge" Event; this event challenges mayors and officials from the state of Texas to climb trees during the State Tree Climbing Competition. Steve Houser is a Tree Climbing Champion and had the "Steve Houser Award of Excellence" (a.k.a. "The Houser Cup") named in his honor; it is awarded each year to the Texas state tree-climbing champion by the International Society of Arboriculture, Texas Chapter. Photo provided by Steve Houser.

This old polaroid photo taken by Steve Houser, shows the remnants of the Trail Marker Tree that stood in Gateway Park and was recognized by the Comanche Nation. Photo provided by Linda Pelon and Steve Houser.

to acknowledge archeological evidence of our past and takes great pride in knowing that the Indian Marker Tree is a living monument to our historic presence in the Great State of Texas..." The article published in 1941 by the Dallas Archeological Society and the efforts by the Texas Forest Service and Comanche Nation have helped to increase the awareness and interest of the Trail Marker Trees throughout the state of Texas.

Unfortunately, little remains of the Trail Marker Tree that stood at Gateway Park, the once great monument to the Comanche Nation. Steve Houser was able to use his 'calculated estimate method' to determine the approximate age of this tree to be 500 years old. Houser created a method to determine approximate tree age without inflicting any damage to the tree by increment boring. The increment boring method literally bores a hole, about a quarter of an inch in diameter, all the way to the center of the living tree. Houser and the author both strongly agree that it is not in the best interest of these historical trees to use increment boring to determine the age of the trees when other methods are available. Houser's calculated estimate method has been written about by Carolyn Bush, Master Gardener, and published in the *International Society of Arboriculture Newsletter* as well as the *Dallas County Master Gardener Association Newsletter*.

Two additional examples of Trail Marker Trees verified by Linda Pelon were also located within the Dallas County area. One tree was located within the California Crossing Park and indicated a ford (an area of low water and safe crossing)

that was used by the Indians and later by the pioneers and settlers. This Trail Marker Tree was a pecan tree. The other tree, a burr oak, located within the same area, was on top of a high escarpment ridge above the Trinity River and pointed to an important quarry that provided the Indians with pigmented rock. The Native American's used this pigmented rock to create natural paints. The groups and individual Trail Marker Tree advocates in the state of Texas have made great efforts to preserve these historical trees in the past and continue to make strides towards their preservation into the future.

Chapter Fifteen

COLORADO

Colorado also has a rich Native American history that dates back as far as 11,500 BC when the Clovis culture inhabited the area. Shortly after, the Folsom culture lived in the area. Both the Clovis and Folsom cultures were big game hunters and were identified by archeologists based on the style of their spear points. However, very little evidence is left of these cultures. Many millennia later, the Pueblo people would leave behind hundreds of cliff dwelling sites at Mesa Verde that would carry on their legacy long into the future.

In 1906, Theodore Roosevelt had the foresight to declare Mesa Verde a national park, "...*to preserve the works of man*." Today, there are over 4,000 known archeological sites that are protected by the Mesa Verde National Park. Other Native American tribes that inhabited the area are the Apache, Arapahoe, Bannock, Cheyenne, Comanche, Jicarilla, Kiowa, Navajo, Shoshoni, and the Ute. Colorado continues to protect numerous Native American archeological sites throughout the state.

In the 1990s, the author began frequenting the Aspen area to visit Janice and Kevin Kozie, originally from Wisconsin. The Kozie family was familiar with Dennis' work and studies. The author was able to meet gallery owner Barney Wyckoff and other art professionals in the Aspen area, and was invited back to do a number of exhibits and private shows. Downes showed some of his interpretive Native American artwork at the famed Toklat Gallery near the Maroon Bells. These experiences gave him the opportunity to discuss his studies on the Trail Marker Trees with a number of Colorado residents.

Howard and Pauline Morrison live in Arrowhead, Colorado, near Vail. However, the Morrison's first met the author in the Midwest and had seen his Trail Marker Tree exhibits as well as his artwork that had been inspired by his time in Aspen, Colorado. The Morrison's invited Dennis to their home in Arrowhead to personally deliver a painting they had purchased. During this trip, the Morrison's introduced Dennis to John Cogswell, owner of Cogswell Gallery. This introduction led to a yearly 10-day show at Cogswell Gallery where the author was able to display his newly casted bronze Trail Marker Tree sculpture, several Trail Marker Tree paintings, and Colorado landscapes. Rie, of Rie Design, attended one of the shows at Cogswell Gallery and would later commission Dennis to paint the Ring of Brodgar in the Orkney Islands, just off the northern coast of Scotland. The author had previously studied the use of upright stone monuments appearing in the Eastern United States and Western Europe. In the United States, the Native Americans used these upright stones as navigational markers along their paths, trails, and rivers, as well as boundary markers. During the same time period, Downes' cousin, Dr. Jane Downes, was working on several archeological sites in the area, including the Ring of Brodgar. Starting in 1999, every year during his show at Cogswell Gallery, the author was featured on *Good Morning Vail* and interviewed by Lynda Gustafson. The yearly show and TV appearances gave Downes many opportunities to expose the area to his study of the Trail Marker Trees from both an artistic and educational point of view.

During an interview with Lynda Gustafson, Dennis was asked if he personally had any ties to the Vail area. In fact, decades earlier, Dennis' uncle, Luis Berriochoa, was part of the 10th Mountain Division and selected to be one of the ski instructors at Camp Hale. After the interview, Dennis was escorted to the Colorado Ski Museum, located in Vail, where he was able to locate his uncle's name documented as part of the 10th Mountain Division. The following day, the Morrison's took Dennis on an ATV tour of Camp Hale, where his uncle had lived and trained.

page 247

The author shown in this scenic shot of the Maroon Bells. This location study and others resulted in the inspiration for many of his Colorado landscape paintings. Photo taken by Janice Kozie.

This photo was taken by the author while hiking with the Morrison's just outside of Vail.

Janice Kozie and a friend taking the author on a hiking trip above Crater Lake in Colorado.

Dennis and his sister, Maryann, in Indian Hill, Colorado preparing for their trip to the Florissant Fossil Beds National Monument Park during an unexpected blizzard.

The author's sister, Maryann Downes, hiking in the National Monument Park, the Garden of the Gods in Colorado.

In the late 1990s, the author was contacted by the owners of a retreat center in the Black Forest area. They had heard his lectures about the Trail Marker Trees and thought they had some Trail Marker Trees on their property. Downes made a special research trip to their area to investigate theses possible Trail Marker Trees. During the trip, Downes found that the trees in this part of the country were not like the Trail Marker Trees he had previously documented and he began to do more research to learn about the American Indians and their practices in this part of Colorado. Through his research, he found that the Ute Indians used trees for several sacred purposes, and some of these trees included Prayer Trees, Medicine Trees, and Burial Trees. According to author Celinda Reynolds Kaelin, during journeys, the Prayer Trees were tied down parallel to the ground as saplings by the Utes. The people would then gather around the tree, pray, and then continue on their journey. These trees would grow into a bent shape very near to the ground, distinguishing them as sacred Prayer Trees.

Another documented use of trees by the Ute is the use of Medicine Trees. Medicine Trees have been well documented starting in the 1800s. The Utes would cut and peel strips of the inner bark of pine trees and eat them for medicinal purposes, often during healing ceremonies. Pine trees with large pieces of bark peeled off can be seen throughout the Pike's Peak area and are regarded as remnants of the Ute Culture. There are other documented uses of trees by the Ute common to the Pike's Peak region recorded by Celinda Reynolds Kaelin.

The author being interviewed by 9 NEWS, KUSA-TV, about one of his research art pieces that he donated to the Friends of Airlife annual Memorial Park fundraiser. The Friends of Airlife nonprofit organization was co-founded by Jim Ulrich, longtime friend of the author. Since that time, the James Alan Ulrich Scholarship Award and the Jim Ulrich Silver Falcon Award have been named in honor of Jim Ulrich for his years of dedication and contributions to Emergency Medical Services. The author donated to and attended this event for several years.

Dennis shown near the triple trunk Trail Marker Tree in the Florissant Park area shown to him by Park Ranger, Phyllis Hochstepler. This Trail Marker Tree designated a Ute campsite and nearby freshwater spring. Photo taken by Maryann Downes.

Howard and Pauline Morrison hiking with the author near Arrowhead, Colorado. Photo taken by the author.

Park Ranger, Phyllis Hochstepler standing with the author's sister, Maryann Downes in front of a giant petrified redwood stump before heading out to research the culturally modified trees in the area. Photo taken by the author.

The author snowshoeing up to a cave in the mountains outside of Avon with friend and local, Terry Kausch, to investigate possible pictographs.

An example of one of the culturally modified, Prayer Trees, shown to the author by Park Ranger, Phyllis Hochstepler. These Prayer Trees appear along known routes of the Ute Indians in the Pike's Peak region. Photo taken by the author.

On Downes' fourth research trip to the Pike's Peak area, he was able to view many of these trees that were culturally altered by the Ute Indians.

Several Colorado residents contacted Downes about possible Trail Marker Trees in the Florissant Fossil Beds National Monument Park area after previously seeing his exhibits or hearing his lectures. Before planning another research trip to the area, Downes contacted his sister, Maryann Downes from Indian Hill, and asked her to visit and investigate the area. Maryann was able to make two trips to the Florissant Park area and gather information for Downes regarding several trees. Downes was able to get in contact with park ranger, Phyllis Hochstepler and made arrangements to travel to the park and surrounding areas. During the visit, Downes was able to meet with Phyllis and she took him through the park, showing him numerous examples of the culturally modified Ute trees, including the Prayer Trees and Medicine Trees. Phyllis and her husband Harry also took Downes to see a documented triple trunk Trail Marker Tree. This triple trunk tree was said to have marked a Ute campsite and a natural spring. Toby Wells, a local historian, grew up near this tree and actually spoke with a Ute Indian woman about the tree's significance. Marilyn Martorano, an archeologist and expert in the area, has also been studying the culturally modified trees in this area for 25 years. Through the efforts of park rangers, local historians, and experts, the culturally modified trees in Colorado are becoming recognized and protected.

Chapter Sixteen

IOWA

Some of the earliest descriptions of Iowa coming from explorers and pioneers focused on the lush green grasslands and beautiful rolling hills. Iowa's landscape varies from steep and rolling hills, to cliffs and caves, to valleys and marshes, and even dense forested areas. This state is bordered by two major, navigable rivers, the Mississippi and Missouri River, and has numerous other river systems running throughout the state. In ancient times, the Native Americans would use the river systems for transportation routes in addition to the many foot paths and trails. Some of earliest tribes in Iowa during the Woodland Period include the Hopewell, Oneota, Glenwood, and Mill Creek.

The Woodland Period Indians left behind many effigy mounds, including the Great Bear Mound that is 137 feet long and 70 feet wide. Later, at the time when the Europeans arrived, the Ioway, Sauk, Mesquaki, Sioux, Potawotomi, Oto, and Missouri tribes were all present throughout the area.

The author has been researching Trail Marker Trees and Native American history in the state of Iowa for a number of years. Ward and Jacky Budweg, of Decorah, initially told Dennis about Trail Marker Trees they had seen in Decorah and the northeastern part of the state, prompting the author to begin his research in that area. The Budwegs had been to the author's Trail Marker Tree exhibits in the Midwest and started watching for the trees during the many bicycling rides they participate in throughout their state and abroad, including the Register's Annual Great Bicycle Ride Across Iowa (RAGBRAI). During a research trip to the area, it was recommended that Downes contact Jerome Thompson, state curator and historic sites coordinator of the State Historical Society of Iowa. Thompson was able to further refer the author to Lynn Alex, director of education and outreach, University of Iowa and Office of the State Archaeologist. Alex was able to get the author in contact with Leah Rogers, archaeologist and architectural historian of Tallgrass Historians L.C. Rogers informed the author about the Old Red Rock Indian Line Sycamore Tree south of Des Moines. This ancient tree was a recognized landmark to the area and served as the boundary line marker for the Sauk and Mesquaki

Indians. Lynn Alex also made a huge impact in helping to spread the word about Downes' study by sending out emails to numerous professionals in the education, historical, archeological, conservation, and forestry fields. Because of Alex's initial efforts, the author received numerous contacts from professionals across the state that helped him find historical references to Trail Marker Trees and Marker Trees as well as living examples.

One of the most well documented historical trees in Iowa is referred to as the "H Tree." The author was contacted by a number of individuals regarding this grafted "H Tree" including Steven Lewka, director of the Story County Conservation Board; Jerry Keys, the environmental education coordinator for Story County Conservation; and Linda Meyers. Linda's brother Dale Hughes was the author of *Milford Township and Proud of It,* co-authored by Jurine Borton. Marilyn Webster, president of the Story County Historical Society, also provided the author with several old references to the "H Tree." A photograph of the "H Tree" was shown in the 1911 book, *A History of Story County, Iowa* by W.O. Payne. This historical Marker Tree was grafted together by the Indians in the 1700's out of a red elm and a white elm. This grafted tree was located along the east bank of the Skunk River, just south of Story City. The "H Tree" would have served as a Marker for the Native Americans. It marked the river access point and made it clear where to get onto or depart from the Skunk River. Grafted trees were often used as Markers to pass along information to the American

This photo of the hickory Trail Marker Tree was submitted by Jerry Keys, the Environmental Education Coordinator for Story County Conservation. Based on the slow growth rate of hickory trees, the tree is estimated to be over two hundred years old.

This photo was taken by the author on the way to meet John Byrd, Area Forester of Shimek State Forest.

Dennis pictured with Jessica Flatt, Area Forester of the Stephens State Forest, standing by the non-traditional Trail Marker Tree located in Stephens State Forest.

Indians, such as departure points along navigable waterways. This concept was confirmed by Helen Hornbeck Tanner during a personal interview with the author. The tree stood as a significant landmark to the surrounding areas for centuries. Unfortunately, it died years ago due to Dutch elm disease. A section of the trunk, cut by Steven Lewka, is preserved in a small museum in Story City.

In Polk County, on the Des Moines River, there is a large, living Trail Marker Tree. The author was first contacted by Mark Dungan, the natural resources manager for Polk County Conservation, about this tree. Dennis also received information from Jerry Keys, the environmental education coordinator for Story County Conservation, and Lori Allen. With directions from Dungan and Keys, the author was able to locate this white oak Trail Marker Tree during a research trip. The tree is high up on the trail overlooking the Des Moines River, where today there is a bridge crossing close by. This non-traditional Trail Marker Tree holds a shape very similar to many other Trail Marker Trees found throughout the Midwest. After documenting this tree, Downes was also contacted by Julia McGuire, a nature enthusiast, after she had seen the tree with her children. McGuire had read about Downes in an article that appeared on the 1000 Friends of Iowa website. 1000 Friends of Iowa is a nonprofit organization that promotes responsible development to conserve and protect natural resources.

In the same area as this non-traditional Trail Marker Tree, there are two traditional Trail Marker Trees, also along the Des Moines River.

The nearest oak Trail Marker Tree was located by the author during his research trip. This tree, however, is on private property and could not be photographed. The other traditional tree was located a bit further on Army Corp of Engineer property. This hickory Trail Marker Tree was located and photographed by Jerry Keys. Downes plans to visit this tree during his next research trip to the area.

South of Polk County in the Stephens State Forest, there is another non-traditional Trail Marker Tree. This white oak tree was located by Jessica Flatt, Area Forester of the Stephens State Forest. Flatt contacted the author after receiving an email about his research that was sent out to all Iowa D.N.R. foresters. Downes was able to meet with Flatt during a research trip to Iowa, where she took him out in the forest to document the Trail Marker Tree. This tree bore a strong resemblance to the non-traditional Trail Marker Tree the author had documented on an earlier trip to Polk County. Later, during the same research trip, Downes traveled further south to meet with John Byrd, Area Forester of the Shimek State Forest. Byrd also contacted the author through email about the traditional Trail Marker Tree he had located in the Shimek State Forest, near Indian Lake. Downes was able to photograph and document this oak tree with Byrd. Both Flatt and Byrd agreed with Downes about the importance of educating children about the Trail Marker Trees to help interest them in their natural surroundings and to get them more involved in the outdoors.

During the author's next research trip to Iowa, he was able to research areas recommended to him by Ulf Konig, park manager of Geode State Park. Konig contacted Downes about three traditional Trail Marker Trees in Iowa; he had located trees in Maquoketa Caves State Park, Geode State Park, and near Green Island. The traditional, oak Trail Marker Tree near Green Island is located atop a bluff overlooking the Mississippi River. The tree located in Geode Park was also an oak and was in an isolated area of the park also atop a bluff, overlooking a tributary that empties into the Skunk River. The Maquoketa Caves State Park is an area of natural beauty that would have been very significant to the ancient Native Americans. Numerous ancient artifacts were found in the caves and throughout the park area to indicate the Native American inhabitation hundreds, even thousands of years ago. Downes was able to spend time hiking and researching the entire park area to better understand the significance of the site. The author was unable to meet with Konig due to a timing conflict and hopes to return in the near future. However he was able to see a possible cedar Trail Marker Tree located atop a bluff in the park that needs further research. Konig continued to contact the author with information and photos and was very helpful during the author's study of the area.

The author contacted Cathy Engstrom, director of communications of the Iowa Natural Heritage Foundation to try and find more information regarding the Effigy Mound National Monument and surrounding area. The Iowa Natural Heritage Foundation strives to protect and restore Iowa's land, water, and wildlife. Since their beginning in the 1970s, they have protected more than 120,000 acres of prairies, woodlands, trails, wetlands, and river corridors. Engstrom was able to refer the author to Dale Henning, anthropologist and archeologist. Downes was able to have numerous conversations with Henning during which, Henning confirmed his knowledge of Trail Marker Trees in Wyalusing State Park, Effigy Mound National Monument, and the Yellow River area. Henning also suggested the author contact the Effigy Mounds National Monument in regards to the research and works of Ellison Orr. Orr was an impressive man who worked during his life as a farmer, teacher, businessman, naturalist and archeologist. He grew up near the Yellow River and the study and documentation of the natural and cultural history of the Yellow River became a life-long project. Orr's retirement, he mapped and documented archeological sites across the state of Iowa, including the Effigy Mounds along the Yellow River. Orr is considered one of the founding figures in Iowa archeology. Henning believed that Orr would have kept a documented record of the Trail Marker Trees in Iowa as part of his many papers. Orr's papers were donated to the Effigy Mounds National Monument after his death. The author contacted the Effigy Mounds National Monument to research Orr's papers and collections and was able to speak with David Rambow. Rambow, also a historian and anthropologist, informed the author that it would be some time before the extensive amount of papers and collections could be organized and reviewed by the staff.

The author was also contacted by Mark Wagner, director of visitor experience of the National Mississippi River Museum, and Mark Edwards, the Iowa D.N.R. trails coordinator, about additional Trail Marker Tree locations. Wagner had known about the Trail Marker Trees for 50 years and had seen them in the Black Hawk Creek Wildlife Area, near Morrison, and in the Jacob Krumm Nature Preserve in Jasper County. Edwards had found a Trail Marker Tree off of a trail near Dubuque. Downes plans to research all of these locations further on his next research trip to the area.

After several of Downes' research trips to the state and many new contacts with state professionals, the author was featured in an article that was published in the *Iowan* Magazine. This article discussed Downes' 30 year study of the Trail Marker Trees and the well-known "H Tree." Andrea and Lee Venteicher contacted the author after seeing this article in the *Iowan* about a Trail Marker Tree located on their property in Allamakee County, bordered by the Yellow River. Their property is protected by a conservation easement created through the Iowa Natural Heritage Foundation. This ancient tree has stood on this land for centuries and, thanks to the efforts of people like the Venteicher's and the Iowa Natural Heritage Foundation, it will be protected for generations to come. The author received an overwhelmingly positive response from the state of Iowa to aid him in his study. Thanks to the efforts of the many individuals and groups mentioned, there is a greater awareness of these culturally modified landmarks left by the Native Americans throughout the state and an interest in protecting them for years to come.

Conclusion

One of the major goals of this book is to draw positive attention to part of our country's history. Through educating people about the few remaining culturally altered living landmarks, more trees may be located and protected. Educating children about these Native American Trail Marker Trees, another goal of this book, will help to increase their awareness and appreciation of nature as well as that of their country's history. Hopefully in the future, shaping and using these Trail Marker Trees as signage throughout parks and nature preserves will be a truly green concept that will last centuries into the future.

This photograph was taken by Dennis during his trip to the ancient Native American site at Maquoketa Caves State Park.

Andrea Venteicher pictured next to the Trail Marker Tree on their property bordering the Yellow River. Photo taken by Lee Venteicher.

Authors Notes

I would like to make it clear that in a book this size it was impossible to give attention to every trip that I took during the course of this study. My trips numbered in the hundreds, from short trips of only a few hundred miles to trips all the way to British Columbia and back. I looked at each trip as a learning experience and an adventure. During the trips, I did not use cell phones or GPS and I found that I tended to pay more attention to the areas I was in with greater detail. I met local people and had one-on-one conversations regarding the local Native American history and the Pioneer history. I visited nature centers, historical sites, and museums and talked with the individuals running these establishments, which gave me an insight to the different needs of individuals in the past living in each and every area. As in all extended outdoor re-search projects, Mother Nature always managed to throw a few curves. Whether it was serious infections caused by lone star ticks, or severe cases of poison ivy covering faces and causing eyes to swell shut, or ice storms in the foothills of Arkansas making travel impossible for days, or being turned back by floods in Missouri, or seeing the fury of raging forest fires in Montana and Canada, or being caught in blinding blizzards in Colorado. There where interesting meetings with poisonous snakes, large dogs, and some scary local characters, all of which were intensified by the fact I was alone on the majority of the trips. Having my power steering go out coming down a mountain, my transmission fail in the foothills of

North Dakota, and stones flying through my windshield were all part of the adventure. Along the way I was able to stay as the houseguest of a local mechanic and even be put up by a local Ranger's family. I hope all of the people who were so helpful to me understand that everything about this adventure could not be shown in the book and that all of the individuals could not be mentioned. But, for the part they played I simply would like to say thanks. I kept my promise of not having a cell phone until this project was completed. With the book completed, I purchased my first cell phone and tested it out during my drive to Boise, Idaho; they are handy little gadgets. To those who have supported my career as a painter and sculptor, thank you; I have completely funded this project from the beginning and your support helped me to continue. Thank you one and all for your continued support